BOMPA

Donna Gassett

Johnnie—

So grateful for your friendship over the years — and for your help! You radiate the joy of Jesus!

Love,
Donna

"LFW"
Let's finish well.

BOMPA

THE LIFE AND LEGACY OF JOHN PARSCHAUER

Donna Gassett

Evergreen Communications, Ohio

Copyright © 2012 Donna Gassett

All rights reserved. No part of this publication may be reproduced, stored in a retrieval system, or transmitted, in any form or by any means, electronic, mechanical, photocopying, recording, or otherwise, without the prior written permission from the author.

The Holy Bible, New International Version®, NIV® Copyright © 1973, 1978, 1984, 2011 by Biblica, Inc.™ Used by permission. All rights reserved worldwide.

Scripture taken from the New King James Version, as noted by (NKJV). Copyright © 1982 by Thomas Nelson, Inc. Used by permission. All rights reserved.

Scripture taken from the New Living Translation, as noted by (NLT). Holy Bible, New Living Translation copyright © 1996, 2004, 2007 by Tyndale House Foundation. Used by permission of Tyndale House Publishers Inc., Carol Stream, Illinois 60188. All rights reserved. New Living, NLT, and the New Living Translation logo are registered trademarks of Tyndale House Publishers.

First published in 2012 by
Evergreen Communications
11288 Alameda Drive
Strongsville, Ohio 44149

ISBN: 978-0-9841560-2-3

All photos are property of the author or used with permission to the author.

Printed in the United States

First Edition

DEDICATION

Years ago, our mother, Maureen Parschauer, started to put Dad's story down on paper. She purposely kept herself out of the pages, but Dad would be the first to acknowledge the crucial role that Mother played in that story!

The love of his life and partner in marriage and ministry for 48 years, she stood faithfully by his side, strong in encouragement and joyful in spirit. Mother of five children and "Nana" to 10 grandchildren, she nurtured the family by creating an atmosphere of warmth and fun. There was a vitality and attentiveness in Mother that inspired those around her. She became a spiritual mentor to her children and also to hundreds of Bible school students who loved her for her listening ear, her hospitality, and her heartfelt wisdom.

I have been honored to finally complete what began in Mother's heart…and I dedicate this account to her and to the God she lifted up and celebrated so faithfully.

ACKNOWLEDGEMENTS

My heartfelt thanks to each family member for contributing in significant ways to the writing of this book.

As the beloved first-born, Sharon (Parschauer-Harder) has been far more than a great memory-keeper of Dad's life story. She and I were blessed by sharing in Dad's ministry from the time we were little girls, singing and harmonizing together to his guitar accompaniment. On the way home from meetings, I would typically fall asleep in the back seat of the car, but Sharon would be up front next to Dad navigating and keeping him company. That scenario would symbolize the relationship of mutual trust, support and love they always enjoyed. And so, Sharon's input into the account of Dad's life has been particularly valuable.

My brothers, John Jr. and Ken have given their generous support and encouragement throughout the project. Ken also came up with the book's title and the cover photo of Dad; John helped manage the production. I am so grateful to you both.

Darlene (Parschauer-Schroeder) brought her unmatched gift of loving discernment to the editing table, along with cups of good hot Irish tea! Thank you, Schwesterlein.

And I could weep in gratitude for my dear husband, Bill, who freed me up to write by serving in all kinds of domestic ways…and always with joy!

To Sonja, daughter, friend, and adviser: your interest in this project has grown into a passion for honoring Bompa and his legacy. Thank you, dear girl o' mine, for all your helpful suggestions and for your gentle prodding to finish the book.

Thanks to Erin Bunting, for helping to edit and for caring about the story.

Special thanks to graphic designer, Anna Welch (Zanotti), of American Policy Roundtable, for overseeing the project with such care, patience, and attention to detail.

TABLE OF CONTENTS

Dedication v
Acknowledgements vii

Introduction 1

CHAPTER 1
From Russia With Faith 3

CHAPTER 2
Matilda's Prayer 11

CHAPTER 3
Life-Changing Decisions 19

CHAPTER 4
Ministry In New Brunswick 25

CHAPTER 5
A Wider Vision 31

CHAPTER 6
The Great Family Adventure 41

CHAPTER 7
German Bible School Grows. . . And Grows 47

CHAPTER 8
God's Way Up Is Down 55

CHAPTER 9
God-Sized Challenges 63

CHAPTER 10
Transitions 69

CHAPTER 11
For This I Have Jesus 73

CHAPTER 12
Dad's Last Battle 81

Epilogue 97

"…Who am I, O Sovereign Lord, and what is my family, that you have brought me this far?"

2 Samuel 7:18 (NIV)

INTRODUCTION

Sometimes it's a symphony; sometimes it's a whistle. Both can have a great lasting impact.

Many remember the life of John Parschauer as a symphony, a grand opus of faith. He trusted God for miracles. As a pioneer missionary, he helped found and direct three Bible schools—one in Canada and two in Germany. He led with integrity and grace for more than 50 years of ministry, and God used him in remarkable ways. He is considered by many as one of the leading Christian leaders of the 20th century in Germany.

We, his kids, heard the symphony, but mostly we heard the whistle and loved it. He whistled when he went about his work—a low, breathy whistle. It was the simple things that made him great to us. He'd walk down to the Saint John River bank to pick fiddleheads with us; he'd stop the car to play hide and seek with us; he'd help our brothers build a go-cart; he'd whittle slingshots; he'd wake us up early for a walk in the woods; he'd have one of us hop in the car with him to do an errand; he'd tell us to "keep your eyes open for deer." He learned to braid my poker straight hair. He taught us to sing and harmonize and accompanied us with guitar.

Often, on ministry tours, Dad would include a short autobiography—his "life story." I remember the thrill of anticipation I felt each time Dad started off with his characteristic dry humor, "I was born in Russia *years and years* ago!" I never tired of hearing his riveting account of God's miraculous protection and provision. The psalmist encourages us to record stories like this "for future generations, so that a people not yet born will praise the Lord" (Psalm 102:18; NLT).

That's why I'm putting John Parschauer's story on paper for you; some of it as I remember him telling it, some of it from the unfinished manuscript on Dad's life that Mother (Maureen Parschauer) entrusted to me, and some of it from my own experience as one of his five children. His first grandchild, our daughter, gave him the name "Bompa," and the name stuck!

So may I introduce to you, "Bompa!"
Listen for the symphony.
Listen for the whistle.

CHAPTER 1
FROM RUSSIA WITH FAITH

Henry and Matilda Parschauer, our grandparents, were among the many German immigrants living in Ukraine at the end of the 19th century. Invited by the Russian czar, Catherine the Great, foreign farmers who were willing to work the rich, undeveloped Russian soil received land in exchange for their labor. To entice these laborers to come, the government made promises that included freedom of religion and exemption from military duty. The opportunity seemed too great to pass up, and so our grandfather left Germany and finally settled in the German-speaking Mennonite village of Walujewka in Ukraine.

Life in Walujewka was harsh and demanding, even for those who weren't afraid of long hours and hard work. Grandpa was determined to give his children a better life than he'd had growing up. He was also determined to do his best for his wife, Matilda, who was born in Odessa. Orphaned at the age of nine, Matilda was forced to quit school in order to go to work. After marrying Henry, she worked beside him, tilling the resistant soil and harvesting the crops.

Her primary responsibility and true joy was nurturing and raising their three children—two daughters and a son, Henry Jr. She sewed their clothes, knitted their sweaters, cooked their meals, and prayed for their souls.

Grandpa was driven by a passion to earn the money and materials needed to provide for his growing family's physical needs. He became the proud owner of a flour mill (a mark of distinction and success), and in time, another mill was added. When steady winds blew over the Russian flatlands, Grandpa stayed at his windmills day and night, sometimes falling asleep from exhaustion while eating his dinner. Grandma Matilda's protests of "It's not worth it, Henry! You're going to kill yourself!" were lost in the prevailing winds where Grandpa saw his opportunity for making a better life.

But stronger winds were soon buffeting their cottage. A diphtheria-like disease claimed the lives of their 5- and 3-year-old daughters within a single week. After digging two tiny graves, Henry and Matilda were stunned to see the same dreaded symptoms developing in 7-year-old Henry Jr. Overwhelmed at the thought of losing all three of her children, Grandma threw herself sobbing onto the floor and begged God to spare their son. In desperation, Grandpa hitched up the horses while Grandma bundled up delirious little Henry Jr. They drove to a veterinarian—the only doctor they could find. The veterinarian hesitated but finally succumbed to the tears of a frantic mother and gave the boy an injection. Miraculously, he recovered.

By the time Henry Jr. was 17 and himself tending one of his father's windmills, he had five more siblings—three sisters and two brothers: Louise, Millie, Tina, Willie, and the youngest, John, born December 29, 1912.

WORLD WAR I

At the outset of World War I in 1914, with Germans and Russians in conflict, German immigrants in Russia were no longer considered legitimate citizens but undesirable aliens. Many fit young men were forced into military service, and others were sent to Siberian work camps. Henry and Matilda went mechanically about life, in spite of the mounting fears, nighttime interrogations, and arrests. One day, Grandpa received a government telegram directing him to the city. He told Grandma goodbye, promised to be back the next day, and left. But he never returned. Russian authorities told Grandma her husband had been deported to an undisclosed location in Siberia. He became a prisoner in a work camp in Orenburg in the Ural Mountains.

Overwhelmed with fear and grief, Grandma prayed for divine strength to get her through the days ahead. Despite being uneducated, she had learned to read two books: the hymnal and the Bible. Day by day, she poured out her heart and found comfort and courage in the promises of God.

One night, she was awakened by a violent knocking at the door and shouts commanding someone to ready the horses—the Russian authorities were taking them. My uncle, Henry Jr., bit back tears as he hitched up his own beloved black pony and watched strangers lead it away. As the men left, Grandma asked the question, "When will we have to go?" The stinging reply was flung back, "If not tonight, then tomorrow." With the growing Russian oppression, it would just be a matter of time before she would be deported. And where? Because she was given an option for her destination, either Siberia or Germany, she chose Germany.

Preparing for the move meant selling or giving away everything but the essentials needed for survival, which Grandma bundled up so the older children could help carry them. Seventeen-year-old Henry Jr. reached out to his mother, trying to offer the support and encouragement his father would have given. The atmosphere was tense and unsettled. Days dragged into weeks as Grandma and her six children (our father was a 2-year-old at the time) made do with the barest necessities and waited for notification of their deportation date.

Finally, the Russian officers came with the summons to leave. Grandma had to make her way to the port in Odessa. A boat would be waiting there to take them across the Black Sea to western safety. Grandma, her elderly in-laws, and her children were a pathetic group, each carrying the carefully wrapped bundles that would prove vital to their survival. One bundle contained loaves of bread which Grandma had baked with money hidden inside them. At one point, Russian officers stopped them to search everyone thoroughly (even tearing out the insoles of their shoes) to make sure no money was leaving the country. But Grandma had outwitted them with her loaves of bread stashed with money.

When they arrived at the port, they were told the ship would sail the following day. Emotionally and physically, everyone was exhausted. Great-grandmother had to be carried, and Great-grandfather was leaning heavily on his cane. Grandma found some primitive accommodations in a room nearby. She arranged the bundles and blankets to make everyone as comfortable as possible. As her children slept soundly in the makeshift quarters, Grandma Matilda lay awake. In her heart she called on God for the strength to go on, to soothe her grieving spirit, and carry her through yet another crisis.

Around midnight, Grandma heard a thud that startled her. She went to check it out. Great-grandfather had fallen from his cot and was lying on the floor muttering, "I must die." He did die that night, and Grandma now had the responsibility of arranging a funeral and consoling her grieving family. As a result, the ship on which they were to sail left port without them. But the disappointing delay was part of God's plan in protecting the family from tragedy. That very ship proceeded to sail into one of Russia's own mines. The explosion left no survivors. Great-grandfather's death had saved eight lives.

Once aboard the next ship, Russian officers approached the family for inspection. When they saw Henry Jr., they pointed to him and asked Grandma, "How old is he?" "Eighteen," she told them. The officials declared that he was old enough for army duty and insisted Henry Jr. accompany them. Grandma kissed her tall, gentle son one last time and called out "aufwiederseh'n" ("until we meet again") as officers escorted him off. It was the last glimpse she'd ever have of her stalwart son.

Overcome with grief at the loss of her father and her oldest son, Grandma summoned divine courage to comfort her tearful brood. Louise, Millie, and Tina, her daughters, did their best to be strong for their mother and to help take care of their young brothers, Willie and John. With faint hope, Grandma entrusted her unknown future to the God she knew was too wise to make a mistake and who had a plan and a purpose in sparing this family.

Henry Jr., meanwhile, was providentially assigned to the same camp as Grandpa in Siberia. Talking long into the night, Henry Jr. described for his father the traumatic events of the past months and days. He described his sad farewell to the family. With love and admiration, he told of his mother's faith and courage. And so father and son consoled each other until news of the ship's explosion reached them.

Henry Jr. confirmed the name of the ship and the sailing date as the very voyage his mother and the family were scheduled to take. In despair, they visualized the horrors of drowning and realized they would never see their loved ones again. Grandpa later said the news cut like a knife through his heart and that after hearing it, he no longer cared whether he lived or died. Swallowed up in grief, he and Henry Jr. had no way of knowing that thousands of miles away, Matilda was offering praise to God for her family's salvation.

REFUGEES

Grandma and her family crossed the Black Sea safely and traveled north to Steegen, near the free city of Danzig in Prussia. Displaced persons. Refugees with one simple goal: survival.

Grandpa's oldest brother, Gustave, lived there and offered Grandma one room for the whole family. She had six mouths to feed, so she accepted any honest job she could find—even if it meant helping farmers by gleaning in their fields—to provide food for the children. One of the farmers, Herr Dielschneider, gave her a daily meal, most of which she brought home to her children. Desperate for food, stalked by starvation, and emaciated herself, Grandma even had to resort to feeding her family dog meat. My Aunt Louise, at the age of 12, took a job as a maid to help support the family.

At night, the children would study by candlelight, but only for limited lengths of time to save the candles. Getting cooking and heating fuel was an almost impossible challenge, but Grandma showed amazing persistence and ingenuity. She gathered coal that fell off passing railroad cars and collected pieces of wood and even horse droppings to burn as fuel. Months passed, and the family was surviving.

And more than surviving. In spite of the hardships, Grandma tried her best to celebrate the holidays in some memorable way. One Christmas stood out in Dad's mind. Knowing how little they had, the children had prepared themselves for a Christmas without gifts. Usually their mother would try to give each child a plate of goodies—an orange, an apple, a few nuts, and a couple of sweets. But this morning when Dad came downstairs he found not only the Christmas treats, but—wonder of wonders—in the middle of the plate . . . a harmonica!

While little John was learning to play his new instrument, his mother, Matilda, could often be found on her knees, desperately seeking God's mercy in providing her family a way out of their pitiful existence. Nearly five years passed. Her children prayed daily for the return of their father, and their brother, Henry Jr. During recess in the school yard one day, my Aunt Tina left her schoolmates and found a secluded spot under an oak tree. There she knelt down and uttered a simple, direct prayer, "Dear God, please bring Daddy back." Reassured, she jumped up and rejoined her classmates.

A few days later, the family's quiet evening was interrupted by a knock at the door. A bearded man, barefoot and wearing a tattered fur coat, entered cautiously. After a few moments of stunned disbelief, Grandma was swept into the arms of her husband, Grandpa Henry. After almost five years of separation, the children had to be reassured and convinced that the stranger really was their father. Grandpa, too, thought he must be either dreaming or witnessing a miraculous resurrection. He'd been led to the house by the Red Cross, hoping to be reunited with his uncle, convinced that his wife and children had drowned in the Black Sea years ago.

When the excitement subsided, the accounts of God's grace and protection were exchanged. Matilda told how the timing of Great-grandpa's sudden death had saved their lives, and together, they wept. Then, surrounded by his children, Grandpa told of his ordeal.

He, Henry Jr., and five other men had managed to escape from the work camp in Siberia. By night, they traveled through the forest, covering as much ground as they could until they were too exhausted to go on. By day, they hid in the bushes. They offered bribes to farmers for information about where the Communists were so they could plan alternate routes. Suspicious that one such farmer was directing them into the hands of Communist guards, the group chose not to follow his advice. It was a mistake in their judgment, and soon the seven men found themselves face to face with the soldiers they'd been trying to avoid. When questioned by the guards about where they were headed, the men told the truth: that they wanted to join their families in Prussia. Four of them were allowed to go on. The two youngest, including Uncle Henry Jr., were detained and sent back to the work camp.

After being wrenched from his son, Grandpa said, "I didn't feel like going on without Henry, but somehow I did." For months, through cold nights, wearing worn-out shoes and a tattered old coat, he kept walking. Several times, soldiers shot in their direction and kept them running.

Once he reached Prussia, he contacted the Red Cross for help in locating his brother, never believing his search would lead him to the doorstep of his beloved wife and children.

Grandma Matilda grieved at the thought of her son, alone in a Siberian camp. She blamed herself for forcing God's hand into healing Henry Jr. of his childhood diphtheria. "Maybe it was God's will to take him back then," she thought. "He would have been spared the pain he's suffering now." With her son just a prayer away, and her husband's arm around her, she sighed deeply and surrendered her regrets to the higher purposes of a sovereign God.

CHAPTER 2
MATILDA'S PRAYER

Reunited, the Parschauer family was invited to live with Ferdinand, Grandpa's youngest brother, who lived in Herdecke, near Hagen, on the Ruhr River in Germany. Grandpa found a job in a local electrical shop. Dad's sisters—Millie, Louise, and Tina—were young women determined to help share responsibilities wherever they could. They helped with the support of the family by taking any small jobs they could find. They also kept their watchful eyes on 10-year-old Willie and 7-year-old John, who spent long, carefree hours exploring the rolling hills and banks of the river.

But life in Germany was hardly carefree. Sometimes gunfire would send the children scurrying to hide in alleys or running home to safety. Not fully realizing the danger, the children thrived on the excitement. Their parents, however, were tense and troubled. Unrest and talk of revolution permeated their conversations. After the children were in bed, Matilda and Henry would talk late into the night, discussing their options for the future and how best to provide a peaceful environment for their growing children. Silently, Grandma prayed for God's guidance.

An answer came in the summer of 1922. Another of Grandpa's uncles, Uncle Albert, sent a letter inviting the whole family to join him in western Canada. He had secured a loan for $1,000 to cover the cost of the ship's fare. In November, packed up once again, our grandparents made plans to take a train to Hamburg. An exchange of gunfire sent them scurrying for cover as they approached the train station. But they finally arrived safely in Hamburg, where they would board a steamship for Canada.

Seeing the ship that would carry them to the "land of promise," the children couldn't contain their excitement. They saw only adventure on the horizon. Grandpa and Grandma, with a more realistic view of the challenges, opportunities, and potential disappointments, wavered between apprehension and hope.

After sailing the Atlantic for 13 days, the Parschauer family docked in Quebec, and the seemingly endless second half of the trip across the golden prairies of western Canada began. At the final train stop in Saskatoon, Saskatchewan, our grandparents loaded their children and their luggage onto a farm truck. The temperature was 40 degrees below zero and the truck jostled them, exhausted and cold, over frozen dirt roads to their new home, the village of Middle Lake.

A wave of grateful relief swept over Matilda. Her family was safe and healthy. The country was at peace. God had been good.

Grandpa quickly adapted to the hard work of a farmer's life and was soon able to provide for the material needs of his family and begin repaying his travel debts. Grandma's frail body grew stronger in the warm summer sun. The children worked alongside them, milking the cows and feeding the animals before school, helping with the field work, chopping wood, and doing other chores when they came home.

But farm chores were easy compared with learning the new language.

At school, my father and his siblings were teased for their clumsy speech. When Dad was eight, he protested the mocking by shouting, "Not!" In German, the word "nicht" means both "don't" and "not," and he had chosen the wrong English word. His gaffe sent his schoolmates into gales of laughter, but he survived the embarrassment and soon formed some good friendships. He joined the kids in playing hockey during the long Canadian winters. After a few years of playing, he and Willie organized a pickup hockey team. They couldn't afford hockey gear so they tied Sears and Roebucks catalogs around their legs to serve as shin guards! In spite of their ragamuffin appearance, they started winning against some of the best teams in the area.

EAT, DRINK, AND BE MERRY

In Canada, Louise and Millie married and began families of their own. Meanwhile, Grandma grew concerned that her husband and children seemed to give little thought to spiritual matters. They seemed self-sufficient and intent on pursuing prosperity and pleasure without acknowledging the hand of God in protecting them and providing for them so graciously. On her knees yet again, Grandma sought peace and solace by pouring out her cares to the Lord, praying not only for the health and welfare of her children's bodies, but for their souls as well.

Now teenagers, Dad and his older brother, Willie, couldn't understand their mother's concern. They always treated her with respect. They worked hard on the farm. They simply felt entitled to some freedom and fun.

The brothers' musical ability paved the way to exciting new opportunities. Dad bought a saxophone with the plowing money he'd earned. Within a week, he was playing the instrument at dances, with Willie accompanying him on either banjo or fiddle. When Tina joined them as a drummer along with two other musicians, the Middle Lake Orchestra was born. With his dry sense of humor, Dad was well-suited to the role of master of ceremonies. The band was soon accepting bookings two nights a week, then three, then four.

While her children were out at night, Grandma lay awake, praying. Later, Dad would tell how he, Willie, and Tina would come home in the quiet predawn, drunk, yet sober enough to feel uneasy at the light in the den window that signaled their mother was still up, waiting and praying for them.

For Grandma, it seemed the more she agonized and prayed, the worse her children behaved. Were her prayers in vain, she wondered? Little did she know, in the room next to hers, Dad was often on his knees as well, praying The Lord's Prayer in an attempt to soothe his own troubled conscience. He admitted he sometimes drifted off to sleep mid-prayer, chiding himself for failing to finish when he woke the following day. But any feelings of guilt were suppressed by "life in the fast lane," and he managed to deny the emptiness of soul that was becoming so apparent to his mother.

Dad didn't look upon himself as a pagan. He'd tried religion. He'd been baptized as a baby in Russia, received religious instruction in Germany, and attended confirmation classes in Canada for three years. He'd stood at the front of the church with the rest of his confirmation class and solemnly answered "yes" to the questions the pastor asked: "Do you believe in God the Father, Almighty Maker of heaven and earth? Do you believe in Jesus Christ, God's son, Savior of the world?" His profession of faith had earned him church membership, and for the first time in his life, he participated in Holy Communion.

In spite of his sincerity, however, religion, confirmation, and church membership made little difference in Dad's life or lifestyle. Warnings came. The pastor challenged him to reform. His brother-in-law confronted him, "John, you're going too far!" His mother pleaded and prayed. And deep in his heart, my father wanted to change, but he felt powerless to break the habits that were beginning to destroy him.

ONE HUNDRED MILES FROM HOME

Dad and his father often drove into the city of Saskatoon on farm business. On one such trip, a chain of events unfolded that would radically alter the direction of Dad's life.

Walking down a sidewalk in town, they met an acquaintance of Grandpa's who asked, "Did you know that George Lepp now lives in Dalmeny?" George Lepp! Grandpa could hardly believe that his best friend from Russia was now living just 15 miles away. He and Dad drove the short distance to Dalmeny and soon the two friends were locked in an emotional embrace. George persuaded Grandpa and Dad to spend the night. Dad had little interest in the men's conversation, recalling little of his few years in Russia. So he went to bed, while the two reunited friends reminisced long into the night.

At breakfast the next morning, Mr. Lepp greeted his guests warmly and with an announcement: "It is our custom to have devotions before we eat." Grandpa would admit to Dad later that George's announcement caught him off guard because it seemed totally out of character with the coarse young man he'd known back in Russia. With bewildered curiosity, Grandpa and Dad watched as Mr. Lepp opened the Bible and read aloud with a strong, clear voice. And then he prayed. His prayer was not the familiar, formal, memorized type of prayer my father was used to hearing. Dad admitted peeking to see if Mr. Lepp was reading the prayer. To his amazement, he saw tears streaming down the man's face as he thanked God for reuniting him with his friend after so many years.

During the meal, Dad detected something different in this family, something appealing that he couldn't define. After breakfast, he offered cigarettes to Mr. Lepp and his 17-year-old son, Jake. Both men refused, saying, "No thanks, John. I don't smoke." He thought it odd that the men didn't smoke, especially a young man like Jake, in the prime of life!

After goodbyes and plans to meet again soon, Grandpa and Dad had a lot to talk about on their trip home. The chance encounter had deeply impressed them both, and they were touched by the warm hospitality of the Lepp family. Still, they both admitted they'd felt awkward and a bit uncomfortable with the religious atmosphere in the home.

When Grandma heard that her neighbors from Walujewka were living just one hundred miles away, she was anxious to see them, too. A date was set for a visit. Aunt Millie volunteered to oversee the farm chores for the weekend so the rest of the family could make the trip. "The Lepps are religious now, you know," observed Aunt Tina. With a laugh she added, "It might do us some good."

Matilda wept with joy at the reunion with her old friends. After dinner, Mr. Lepp mentioned that evangelistic meetings were being held nightly at the local school. "Tonight is the last of them. Would you care to go with us?" he asked. Not wanting to offend his host, Grandpa answered for the rest of the family. "We're your guests. We'd be happy to join you."

Years later, Dad admitted he felt uneasy entering the auditorium for his first gospel meeting. Two energetic 20-something preachers, Ed Ericson and Herbert Peeler, shared the platform. And as penetrating as the sermon was that evening, it was a song by a German choir that had the greater impact on our father.

Wenn der Meister wird Dich fragen
Wo has Du dein Pfund?
Was wirst Du als Antwort sagen?
Stumm bleibt dann Dein Mund.

When the Master one day asks you
Where did you bury your talent?
What answer will you give?
Your lips will be silent.

After the meeting, Dad filed out with the crowd. At the door, he felt a touch on his shoulder and turned to face the Lepp's married daughter. With tears in her eyes she asked him, "John, wouldn't you like to go and speak to the ministers?" Almost flippantly, Dad replied, "Well, if they have something to tell me, why not?" Accompanied by his brother, Willie, he went back into the building.

Ed Ericson, the evangelist, invited the brothers to sit down. "John, do you believe that the Bible is the Word of God? Do you believe in a heaven and a hell? Do you know that you have sinned against God?" Dad quickly answered yes to all of Ericson's questions. But then the young preacher asked a question he couldn't answer. "Have you ever been born again?"

Ericson explained to Dad and Willie that to be born again meant to acknowledge that Jesus died on the cross in their place, that they were guilty of sin and deserved to be judged for it, but that Jesus had taken their punishment. He read from John 1:12, "As many as received Him to them He gave the right to become the children of God to those who believe in His name" (NKJV).

"That means you must invite Jesus into your life and receive him as your personal Savior. Then you are born into the family of God," he explained.

Soon, both my uncle and my father were kneeling on the floor, confessing their sin and praying to receive the gift of salvation. Their sister, Tina, was watching from the back of the auditorium. She ran outside and fumed, "My brothers are making fools of themselves. They'll never keep the promise they're making; I know them too well." What she didn't know was the grace of God.

A sensitive bystander noticed Tina's frustration, followed her outside and soon had her engaged in a conversation about her own spiritual condition. Tina's defenses crumbled, and on that warm July night, she, too, knelt and prayed. Her altar was the running board of the Parschauer family's Ford. But her prayer was the same as her brothers': to receive Jesus Christ as her Savior.

Transformed in attitude, Tina joined her brothers and the preacher inside the auditorium for a prayer of thanksgiving.

Back at the Lepps', Grandma was growing anxious. She feared her children had probably left the service to search for more exciting night life in the town of Dalmeny. Mr. Lepp volunteered to drive back to the school to check on them. After peering through the window, he drove back to deliver his report.

"Matilda, your children are on their knees praying!"

No news could have been sweeter. I can only imagine the joy in my grandmother's heart to see the answer to her many years of agonized prayer. All three of her children in one night!

In all the jubilation, Grandpa must have felt left out because later that same evening, after hearing what his children had done and surrounded by caring friends, his resistance to the gospel of Christ finally crumbled, too. Kneeling at the living room sofa with his friend, George Lepp at his side, Grandpa humbled himself before God, admitted his sin and self-sufficiency, and called upon Jesus for salvation.

UNDER PRAIRIE SKIES

Driving home the next day, the family sang hymns all the way! The songs their mother had sung to her family since their childhood suddenly came back into memory, and everyone wanted to sing them.

The day before, on the way to Dalmeny, Dad, Willie, and Tina had stopped to post nine announcements for upcoming dances at which they were scheduled to perform. Now, on the return trip, they stopped to rip them down. When curious bystanders asked why, Dad gave the only answer he could come up with: "Middle Lake Orchestra's busted up!" The Parschauer siblings, whose lives had been radically changed, somehow knew they should no longer be playing for dances; the environment would offer too many temptations.

The telephone kept ringing, however, with friends who wanted to know what had happened. "The band is broken up?" "Why?" "You got religion?" "Are you turning into hermits?" "What about your musical talent?" Dad and Willie argued over who would answer the incoming calls because neither knew how to adequately explain to their friends what had happened. Later, Dad would find the explanation in 2 Corinthians 5:17, "Therefore, if anyone is in Christ, he is a new creation; old things have passed away; behold, all things have become new" (NKJV). His desires and motivations were being transformed by God. Old habits dropped away. Dad never smoked or drank alcohol again.

He and Willie were also infused with a naive belief that if they simply explained the gospel, their friends would eagerly receive the gift of salvation just as they had. Instead, their friends tried to talk them out of their decision by rationalizing, "If all of us can go to hell, why can't you?"

Although the brothers felt at a total loss to answer their friends' questions, they could understand, too. Only a few days before, they were using the same arguments to refute their mother's pleas for them to quit the dance scene and the lifestyle connected with it. Nevertheless, a painful rift began to grow between them and their friends.

In his loneliness, Dad began going into the pasture to meet with God and tell Him everything that was going on. There, under prairie skies, he prayed for strength to be faithful to the commitment he had made to his Savior. Dad would never forget the peace those times of communion brought to his soul. As he would say, "God gave me a song sweeter than any we had sung on the night club stage."

That summer, as he milked cows, plowed fields, and repaired fences, Dad sang and talked with God. He also wrote, telephoned, and met regularly with evangelist Ed Ericson. The young preacher was a constant source of encouragement, and he eventually invited Dad, Willie, and Tina to play their instruments at one of his meetings. What an honor! To be playing the saxophone again but in quite a different setting. As they met hundreds of others who were following and serving Jesus Christ, suddenly, the three siblings didn't feel so lonely.

Ericson strongly urged new Christians to study the Bible and, if possible, attend Bible college for more concentrated training. My father, then 20, took his friend's advice and one fall day packed up his belongings and headed for Millar Memorial Bible Institute, 400 miles away in the tiny village of Pambrun, Saskatchewan.

His emotions were mixed. On the one hand, he was elated at the prospect of studying the Bible. On the other, he was reluctant to leave his family knowing his absence would add to their workload on the farm. As he drove away, he looked back at the home he had helped build—the home that held so many memories. Through tears, he saw his parents standing in the doorway as if in a framed portrait, waving goodbye.

CHAPTER 3
LIFE-CHANGING DECISIONS

The town was so small that Dad said he drove right past Pambrun without even recognizing it. Realizing his oversight, he turned the car around and drove past it again from the opposite direction! Then, in the darkness, he saw a light shining in the valley. He would later describe how, for him, that tiny light represented the spark in his spirit that would be fanned into flame over the next three years.

The Bible school was founded in 1928 by the Scottish pioneer, William Millar. In 1933, Herbert Peeler, a young graduate of the school, joined the staff as his assistant. A godly, humble man, Peeler was uniquely qualified to assume leadership of the school when Millar died a few months later and left him in charge.

Dad was one of the four men in the incoming class. When he saw the primitive conditions of the college, he wondered if he'd been too hasty in turning down an offer of free tuition and board he'd received from an established Lutheran seminary. Dad had no money for supplies; he often prayed for money for stamps so he could write home. Meals that the students themselves prepared consisted of the most basic staples. But they feasted on Scripture as it was carefully presented to them. Dad flourished spiritually under the outstanding teaching at Millar Memorial Bible Institute, and his apprehension about the school dissolved. He'd arrived at the school "biblically illiterate," not even owning his own copy of the Bible. With no idea how to locate specific passages, Dad would flip self-consciously through the pages whenever the teacher cited a reference, often relying on the sympathetic help of his classmates.

Along with classroom training, Dad was challenged and impressed by Herbert Peeler. Still in his twenties, the young college president modeled hard work alongside a zest for playful fun. He'd travel long distances in his truck or on foot to lead gospel meetings, and no day was too cold for a game of hockey. Peeler was an example to his students "in speech, in life, in love, in faith and in purity" (I Timothy 4:12, NIV).

Another influential friend was Dad's roommate, Ken Robins. Dad found he had a lot in common with this tall, lanky fellow bachelor. Buoyant and congenial, Robins, too, had sowed plenty of wild oats until Jesus Christ had transformed his heart and desires. He and Dad became best friends, even helping each other learn to launder their own clothes. Their method? Throw whites and darks into a big pot and boil them all together!

Dad and Ken were always grateful when area families invited them for home cooked meals. Glenn and Margaret Gamble, along with their five children, never seemed to mind adding a place setting or two. Dad enjoyed interacting with young Jack Gamble, and his four lovely sisters. Fifteen-year-old Maureen—petite, outgoing, and quick with a laugh—made an especially strong impression on Dad.

After completing his first year of Bible school, Dad returned home to Middle Lake to work on the farm. He and Willie wanted to hold church services in the public school building. They announced the meetings on the telephone's party line (three rings for a public message). When asked who the speaker would be, Dad and Uncle Willie mustered their courage and answered, "Well . . . it's John!"

A local pastor heard about their plans and questioned their qualifications to preach without seminary degrees. Undeterred, yet respectful of the pastor's concerns, Dad and Willie went ahead with their plans. They were nervous. Would anyone come? As the service time approached, townspeople began arriving, curious to see what had happened to these musicians turned preachers.

The brothers began the service singing and playing their instruments to the glory of God. When Dad began speaking, a man in the audience stood up suddenly and asked a theological question Dad knew he couldn't answer adequately. His face grew warm and his heart thumped in his chest in the tense atmosphere. Then, to his relief, a big burly Dutchman, well-known and respected in Middle Lake, stood up and told the man (later found out to be a cult leader) to "Sit down! We've come here to hear John speak!" He did, and the service went on uninterrupted.

Response to the service was so positive that Dad and Willie held weekly services. And so a local community of believers gathered and grew over the next two years. There was some opposition to the ministry, however, and permission to use the school building was withdrawn. The brothers prayed about a new location, and on their last Sunday in the school, they made an announcement: "Next week, services will be held at a log church." They gave directions to the church and then got busy building it!

Willie supplied the logs—logs he'd intended to use to build a home for himself and his bride, Annie. He and Annie came to the decision together; and so for the first two years of their marriage, they lived in with Grandma and Grandpa Parschauer until Willie earned the house "logs" again. Many others offered their time and help. God honored the brothers' youthful zeal, and the following Sunday, the "Gospel Chapel" opened as promised.

A CALL TO MISSION

During the next two years of Bible college, Dad felt certain God was calling him into missions as his life's work. But where? Everywhere he looked, the need was desperate. China? Japan? South America? Finally, his heart was drawn to Africa. Dad applied to a mission board, and to his surprise, his application was denied. Disappointed, he prayed for God's wisdom and direction about what to do next.

After graduating from Millar Memorial Bible Institute, Dad worked on the farm in Middle Lake, preached regularly in the new chapel, and held area evangelistic meetings. He never charged for his preaching and saw God provide for his needs sometimes in unusual ways. Once, after a longer time in ministry away from home, he needed a train ticket to travel back home for Christmas. A total stranger handed him an envelope; inside it was twenty dollars, more than enough for the trip.

Dad took every opportunity to minister in preaching or in music and rarely went anywhere without his saxophone and guitar. On one train ride, the ticket master noticed Dad's guitar in the overhead luggage rack.

"Why don't you take that thing down and sing and play for us?" he suggested.

"Well, what would you like me to sing?" Dad asked.

"Oh, sing, 'A Hot Time in the Old Town Tonight.'"
Without a word, Dad took the guitar and started singing:

> *I left the way of death and sin*
> *The road that many travel in*
> *And if you ask the reason why*
> *I seek a glorious home on high.*
> *This world, this world is not my home...*

In 1940, Dad accepted an invitation from Briercrest Bible Institute President Henry Hildebrand to join the faculty at the school in Caronport, Saskatchewan. He admired Henry Hildebrand for his wise counsel and administrative skills, warmth and humor, self-discipline, and discernment. Fellow teachers Homer Edwards, Orville Swenson, Od Brygmann, and Abe Cornelson formed Dad's new circle of friends, and he was challenged by the caliber of these men. Still, as much as he enjoyed teaching, he couldn't deny the tug at his heart for foreign missions.

When his third year of teaching came to an end, Dad told Mr. Hildebrand of his growing conviction to pursue foreign missions. Hildebrand graciously supported Dad's decision to leave Briercrest after the spring conference. It was during that very conference that Dad met D.R. Aikenhead, superintendent of the Canadian Sunday School Mission (CSSM). Aikenhead asked Dad to consider going to the Maritime Provinces to help start a CSSM branch in eastern Canada.

The prospect of leaving the security of Briercrest and all that was dear and familiar in the prairie provinces and moving two thousand miles away was daunting. Dad knew no one in the eastern provinces and had been warned that easterners were a cold, conservative group. But God was calling, and knowing He would prepare the way, Dad accepted the invitation.

MAUREEN

When Dad prayed about finding a wife, companion, and partner to share his life and ministry, Maureen Gamble's sunny face kept coming to mind. Maureen was working as a student nurse in Toronto, Ontario, and Dad hoped to see her there on his way to New Brunswick. As the train headed toward Toronto, he found himself growing more and more nervous.

A group of Bible school friends had planned to get together, and Maureen was there. As the evening of fellowship drew to a close, Dad offered to accompany Maureen on the bus back to her dormitory. Not picking up on Dad's romantic intentions, Maureen said another nursing student from her dorm would also be joining them. Dad quickly called a cab for the friend and even paid the fare so he and Maureen could ride the bus alone.

The freckle-faced, 15-year-old girl that Dad remembered from Pambrun had grown into a radiant, intelligent young woman who loved the Lord. But could she possibly learn to love him? He had no financial security and no home yet in New Brunswick. Was it too soon to propose? What kind of life could he offer her? With questions swirling in his mind, at the bus stop, Dad asked Maureen to marry him. He could hardly believe it when she said, "I've always respected you, John, and I would be honored and happy to become your wife."

With a song in his heart, Dad continued on to New Brunswick, to the home of Mr. and Mrs. Clayton Clark. Mr. Clark was a soft-spoken businessman, and his wife's gracious hospitality made Dad feel right at home. The Clarks shared a zeal for evangelism, and Mr. Clark was president of a newly formed Maritime CSSM board. The board laid the groundwork for upcoming summer vacation Bible schools and a summer camp.

In May, Dad took the long train ride back to western Canada and married his dear Maureen Gamble on May 10, 1944. His good friend and former roommate Ken Robins officiated at the ceremony. At the reception, Ken read a telegram that had been sent by a well-wisher: "It's a Gamble, but a good one!"

CHAPTER 4
MINISTRY IN NEW BRUNSWICK

Dad and Mom returned to New Brunswick to face the challenges of ministry together. In a car he borrowed from Mr. Clark, Dad looked for host homes for the vacation Bible schools. He set out for the nearby town of Hartland to find volunteers. At the train station, he noticed a man struggling to fit several cartons of chicks into his car. Dad offered to help transport the chicks to Cloverdale. As a result, he was warmly welcomed into the man's home, and through him, into the community.

He also earned permission to promote the summer camp program in the public schools. To help children who couldn't afford the $5 tuition, a free week of camp was awarded to any child who could memorize one hundred Bible verses.

Soon, Dad had organized his first vacation Bible school. And before long, so many people had offered to host schools in their homes that there weren't enough qualified teachers to lead them! The shortage of teachers was due, in part, to the fact that there was no Bible training center in eastern Canada. The nearest one was one thousand miles away, in Toronto. Dad sent out an S.O.S. to some western Bible colleges, and several students volunteered to help for the summer.

In the fall, Dad's evangelist friend, Ed Ericson, came to join in the gospel meetings in New Brunswick. As more and more young people accepted Christ, Ericson became concerned that there was no Bible school for them to attend. Discussing his concern with my father, Ericson asked, "John, why don't you start a Bible school?" Dad admitted he was startled by the question at first, but the more he pondered the challenge, and the more he prayed, the more convinced he became that he should pursue the possibility.

Dad discussed the idea with Clayton Clark and other members of the CSSM board. As the men deliberated over founding a Bible school, the board treasurer asked the obvious question: "How much money do we have to begin this project?" Summer ministries had drained their funds. Train tickets for the western volunteers were an added expense. It was war time and money was tight. The CSSM had a treasury of $10. It would take a miracle. And the same God who multiplied five loaves and two fish began to provide what was needed.

Mr. Clark offered his vacated Rosedale farm as a site. The small farm house had no electricity, no heat, no running water, and the rooms would need much work to be made ready for students. Nevertheless, Dad and his fellow board members decided to move ahead, trusting in a faithful Lord to open the way step by step. Dad recruited 10 young people for a winter Bible study and willing workers began to join the team. Pambrun Bible Institute graduate Helen Dosso was appointed as dean, with fellow graduate Thelma Orvick serving as cook. Neighbors offered to house students, donate food, and help with transportation; and in October 1944, New Brunswick Bible Institute officially opened.

SNOWBOUND

That winter, it snowed like never before. Snowbound for days on end, the 10 young students had little to distract them from their study of God's Word. Sunday evening services were open to the public, and attendance grew steadily. On weekends, students and staff helped area churches with outreach ministries.

Mom made the best of the primitive conditions at Rosedale. She helped cook for the students and taught English and etiquette. It was her firm belief that for these young people to be effective in ministry, they'd need some social graces to go along with their Bible knowledge!

On Valentine's Day that winter, in the middle of a severe snowstorm, Mom gave birth to my sister Sharon. In his exhilaration and delight, Dad brought his guitar to the hospital and serenaded his baby daughter with the song "Rose of Sharon (So Precious to Me)."

As the winter snows melted, the 10 young students prepared to leave for their summer missions. Most of them joined CSSM as vacation Bible school teachers in rural communities.

GROWING PAINS

Already, Dad felt his new workload was growing beyond his capabilities. He desperately needed godly leaders to share the responsibilities. He immediately thought of his good friend Ken Robins, who was then superintendent of Manitoba's CSSM and teaching at the Winnipeg Bible College.

The New Brunswick Bible Institute board agreed to offer Ken the position of principal. Dad was overjoyed when Ken accepted and arrived with his wife Ruth and their 3-year-old daughter, Kaye. Ken and Ruth jumped right in, leading vacation Bible schools during the summer months as they waited for the fall semester to begin.

The growing ministry would require larger facilities as well. The board purchased a large home on 20 acres overlooking the St. John River in nearby Victoria, and a preconstructed building was moved two miles from Rosedale. The building was winterized and partitioned to include an apartment for the Robins, an office, and a girls' dormitory. Mom and Dad occupied the first floor of the other house and the upstairs became the boys' dorm.

Seventeen students were enrolled for the 1945 fall semester, and the addition of a new freshman class made it necessary to hire another teacher. Dad met Mark Bredin, an assistant pastor at St. Luke's Anglican Church, at a Youth for Christ rally in Halifax, Nova Scotia. When Dad returned home, he told Ken Robins about Mark and they agreed to offer him the teaching position. Later that summer, Mark and his wife Mildred moved to New Brunswick Bible Institute just in time to help plaster the walls of another new dormitory.

A neighboring farmer, Walter Whitehouse, was suspicious of this "religious setup." But he was also impressed by the Bible teachers' willingness to get their hands dirty, saying, "Those preachers sure aren't afraid of hard work." One stormy Friday night, Whitehouse and his wife, Evelyn, attended a prayer meeting at the school. When Dad asked for prayer requests, Evelyn stood up and said simply, "Pray for me. I want to be saved." A year later, after seeing the change in his wife's life, Walter accepted Jesus as well. And a few years after that, the once skeptical farmer was appointed president of the New Brunswick Bible Institute board.

Money was another issue of concern. Because the Bible school was interdenominational, the board couldn't rely on any one organization for its funding. But God provided financially with an ever-growing circle of Christian friends and community members who believed in and supported Bible training for young people.

Dad's heart for missions still burned. And although the school's main emphasis was teaching the Bible, Dad also knew the Good News was meant to be shared and missions would have to become a focus as well.

The school board asked several missions organizations to send representatives to New Brunswick Bible Institute. Two responded, saying they hadn't sent representatives to the area in 13 years. At the beginning of the fall semester, the school hosted its first missions conference, with real live missionaries! Tommy Titcombe and Ed Ratzlaff of the Sudan Interior Mission and John Bell and Raymond Frame of the China Inland Mission inspired and challenged the students, staff, and conference guests.

After the conference, the missionaries visited churches throughout the Maritime Provinces and in Maine, urging congregations to get involved in missions. Many caught the vision and added foreign missions to their budgets.

Of the 10 students in the first New Brunswick Bible Institute graduating class, two became overseas missionaries, and eight served in Canadian churches where they faithfully promoted world missions. Eventually, thousands of local churches were making sacrificial financial pledges to missions, and Dad learned an amazing principle—you can't outgive God.

EXPANSION

The work began growing . . . and growing. As God provided the funds, dormitories, and classrooms, a conference hall and gymnasium were built. In addition, six full-time staff members were added. Fifty-two missionaries led 89 vacation Bible schools, sharing the gospel with more than 20,000 people. And a Bible school correspondence course was flourishing.

In December 1947, Dad wrote in a CSSM newsletter that, "As a mission, we have every reason to praise God for all He has done."

Summertime construction projects made it necessary to find another location for the children's summer camps. A picturesque lakeside location 45 minutes away was purchased, and Dad, Mr. Clark, and several other men trekked across frozen Davidson Lake to clear the land. Eventually, they cleared enough trees to make room for the main building, and "Sandy Cove" was born. The camp became a summer haven for children, many of whom trusted Jesus as Savior during their stay.

In 1951, Dad began producing and directing "The Children's Hour," a live weekly broadcast aired from a radio station in Houlton, Maine. On air, Mom dramatized the "Susie Books," a series of stories with real-life adventure and spiritual application. My sister Sharon was "Susie," and several Bible school students were regulars on the show. Dad provided sound effects, such as a creaking door, a baby's cry or a thunderclap, on his old tape recorder. Once during a suspenseful story, Mom read, "Suddenly, a great clap of thunder broke the stillness." She paused, waiting for the thunderclap. Nothing. Dad had miscued the tape. Mom improvised and tried again. "Then there was another clap of thunder!" Still nothing. By now, Mom was trying so hard not to laugh that tears were spilling down her cheeks as she tried to keep up her dramatic narration . . . without sound effects. Dad told us about the time he set up his recorder in a sheep pen while the cooperative farmer tried to make the uncooperative sheep bleat.

In spite of the bloopers, a regular radio audience of thousands of children grew to include adults as well. Many people wrote letters saying they had received Jesus as Savior after listening to the program.

As Dad and Mom's ministry was expanding, so was their family. In May 1946, Dad drove Mom to Woodstock Hospital where she gave birth to a second daughter: me! Moments after my birth, the doctor assured Mom, "Mrs. Parschauer, you have another healthy daughter." Still groggy on the delivery table, Mom's response was "That's nice. The next one will be a boy." The doctor laughed and joked that not many women start planning for the next one quite so soon!

But Mom was right. Two years later, just before Christmas, the first Parschauer son was born. Sharon and I were thrilled to have him wrapped up under the tree as the best gift we received that year. The next morning, when Dad walked into the classroom to teach, the students were anxious to hear news of the birth. Without a word, Dad picked up a piece of chalk and wrote on the blackboard, "His name is John," just like Zachariah, the father of John the Baptist had announced the name of his miracle son. The room full of young Bible students broke into exuberant applause. A few years later, in 1952, our sister Darlene was born. She soon captivated us all by her happy spirit and charm. I remember seeing her often as a toddler contentedly perched on Dad's lap, his arm encircling her, while he studied at his home office desk.

As busy as he was, Dad took time with us—playing hide and seek, building doll beds, and, at Easter, hiding eggs for us to find in the meadows along the Saint John River.

A bedtime ritual began during those years in New Brunswick. Dad and Mom would gather us all into the living room for short devotions. After Dad read the Bible story to us, we would kneel at the sofa to sing the prayer, a poem by Mary Duncan:

> *Jesus, tender Shepherd, hear me*
> *Bless Thy little lamb tonight*
> *Through the darkness be Thou near me*
> *Watch my sleep till morning light*
>
> *All this day Thy hand hath led me*
> *And I thank Thee for Thy care*
> *Thou hast clothed me, warmed and fed me*
> *Listen to my evening prayer*
>
> *Let my sins be all forgiven*
> *Bless the friends I love so well*
> *Take me when I die to heaven*
> *Happy there with Thee to dwell*

Bless Daddy and Mommy, and Sharon, and Donna, and Johnnie, and Darlene, and everybody (which later would include Kennie and any pet that we happened to own at that time!) . . . *AMEN*

CHAPTER 5
A WIDER VISION

In 1948, a colleague of Dad's from western Canada made an unexpected visit that would dramatically change the direction and course of our lives. Mr. Sinclair Whittaker, board chairman of the Briercrest Bible Institute, had recently made a mission trip to Europe. In Switzerland, Mr. Whittaker had met with the director of Beatenberg Bible School, Dr. Gertrud Wasserzug, to discuss the possibility of pioneering a similar school in Germany. Post-war Europe was in desperate need, and the young people there were experiencing deep spiritual hunger after being disillusioned by Nazism, atheism, and liberalism. Because of Dad's thriving, successful ministry in New Brunswick, his name had come up as the man to lead the way.

"John Parschauer knows the German language. He's had experience at three different Canadian Bible schools and has a heart for mission," Mr. Whittaker had said. "Maybe he is God's choice for directing a spiritual training center for Germany's youth."

Dr. Wasserzug invited Dad to come to Beatenberg the following summer so Dad could help with camp ministries and brush up on his German. In August, he would take part in the International Conference for World Evangelization at Beatenberg, with visiting delegates from all over Europe. "It would provide the perfect opportunity for you to discover if God is either opening or closing doors for outreach within Germany," Mr. Whittaker told Dad.

The offer came like a thunderbolt. "I was perfectly content where we were," Dad would say later. "But I had been teaching the importance of world missions and of being open to God's leading. Could I at least be willing to consider the possibility of going overseas myself?"

The effect such a change would have on Mom and us children was also something to consider. Mom looked realistically at the sacrifices she would have to make and the dangers Dad might be facing by going to Germany alone. All things considered, she gave him her wholehearted support to go ahead and accept the offer to minister in Europe that summer.

Ken Robins, Mark Bredin, and the Bible school board were equally supportive. Even though Dad's departure would place added responsibility on the staff at New Brunswick Bible Institute, the faculty and board voted unanimously to stand behind him if God led him to Germany.

God began to work in amazing ways. Before the end of June, Dad received passage money, the required visas, and peace of heart and mind that God would arrange his schedule and daily needs in war-torn Europe. In July 1949, Dad left Hartland for the town of Juniper and boarded a train for the port city of Halifax, in the province of Nova Scotia. He said my 6-month-old brother John's smile when he kissed him goodbye lived with him the whole summer. So did the sight of Sharon and me, then 4 and 3, waving with Mom from the station until the train turned the bend.

Dad tentatively boarded the 900-foot long *Acquitania*. Past travels had proven Dad wasn't much of a sailor, and he was often plagued by seasickness. But the ocean on this trip was "calm as a mill pond," and an old ship master who'd been on that run for years said he'd never seen the sea so still.

After docking in London and spending some time in both England and France, Dad finally arrived in Beatenberg, the Bible school in the Swiss Alps. He was overwhelmed by the beauty of the country: snow-capped mountains, deep gorges, sheer cliffs, serene lakes, and profuse flowers. At the school, all new guests were welcomed by the dining room waitresses and students singing lovely choruses, first in German and then in English. Meals were preceded and followed by prayer, and the hospitality was courteous and warm.

Dad helped at the youth and children's camps and also attended the International Conference for World Evangelization held on August 6–13, 1949. Three hundred delegates representing 17 countries attended the conference. The experience inspired Dad, and his vision for ministry in Europe quickly expanded. After a month in Switzerland, Dad boarded a train for Germany. As he traveled toward Herdecke along the Ruhr River where he'd spent most of his childhood, he saw firsthand the awful devastation caused by the World War II bombings. His childhood home was badly damaged but still standing. Many who had lived in the city had died of starvation in the war's final stages.

A Wider Vision

While in Europe, Dad had a chance encounter with a man who said he knew the stepson of his brother, Henry. Since Henry's deportation, Dad had heard nothing of his whereabouts. Eventually, the stepson sent the following letter, which shed more light on what had happened to Henry:

> Concerning my father, your brother, I can report the following: On December 11, 1937, the Russians took my father, and since that time there has been no trace of him. All inquiries regarding his whereabouts have been unsuccessful. To this day, I do not know if he is still alive. My brother died on August 17, 1939. In 1943, my mother and three sisters were taken from me and sent to [undecipherable], during which time I was drafted into the army. Since then I have not seen Mother or my sisters again, nor my wife whom I married in 1937, nor my two children. All have been lost to me. I did receive a notice secondhand from my wife dated August 1945, in which she informed me that she and the children found themselves on a Russian transport en route to Siberia. Judging from the circumstances and conditions which reign in such a concentration camp, it is very doubtful if they are still alive.

This heart-wrenching account of our family members was typical of the tragic stories Dad heard day after day during his weeks in Germany. In Herford, he visited a refugee camp and conducted a small outdoor service for the children there. He met a South American family who had been visiting Germany when the war broke out. All three of their sons had been drafted; one was killed, and one was lost somewhere in Russia. The third son had fled back to South America. The parents and their two daughters, who had lost all their earthly possessions, invited Dad to the 6×8 foot room that had been their home for two years. They served a meal of macaroni—no bread, coffee, or anything else—and Dad was humbled by their hospitality and touched by their generosity.

Wherever he went, Dad met people who had been stripped of all material goods but were spiritually receptive. In Hagen, a city 80%

destroyed by war bombings, Dad preached to 1,100 people crowded into a large tent. He spoke again in a Lutheran church, and after he'd dismissed the 300 listeners, nobody moved! So Dad explained the gospel again and invited those who wished to accept Jesus as Savior to meet with him in the parsonage. About 20 adults responded to the invitation.

During his five weeks in Germany, Dad shared in people's sorrow like never before. Some people left an indelible impression on him: Rosa, a deaconess of incredible bravery who helped the sick and destitute during the war, saying, "I was not the least bit afraid because I was protected under the shadow of the Almighty." And then there was the Fussle family: Alfred, a pastor, and his wife, Martha. During the heaviest bombings, they'd huddled with their four small children in a basement corner. When the children began to cry, Alfred prayed and together the family sang songs of praise. Suddenly, a bomb struck their home, demolishing it and filling the basement with debris—all but their one small corner.

One visit to a refugee camp moved Dad deeply. He had been encouraged to go and see a Christian man living there who had lost everything in the war—house, belongings, and his whole family. On the way to the shelter, Dad wondered what he could possibly do or say to encourage a man that destitute. He found him in a small, almost bare room with a single bed, a small table, and, on the table, a well-worn Bible. Before Dad could even say anything, the man started talking of God's blessings in his life. "Mr. Parschauer, I am living every day in the presence of God. Heaven is so real to me; I am experiencing the love of Christ like never before. If God should bless me more than He does, I think I would burst!" Dad left that little room overwhelmed and challenged by the depth of such spiritual comfort and joy. He told us, "I went hoping to encourage a suffering man; instead he encouraged and inspired me."

The summer ministry came to a close and Dad returned to Canada changed and grateful for all he'd experienced. Somehow, God had allowed him to minister and lead many to Jesus. Still, at that time the prospect of founding a Bible institute seemed overwhelming, if not impossible.

Back home, Dad resumed teaching and supervising the Canadian Sunday School Mission. But that winter, Europe beckoned again.

Youth for Christ International was recruiting young people for one hundred evangelical teams to visit Europe during the summer of 1950. Dad admitted he wasn't ready to return to Europe so soon. The harsh realities of his last summer in Germany were still fresh in his mind. But Mr. Clark persisted. The young volunteers wouldn't know the German language or have any mission experience. Dad had both.

He and Mom prayed. Faculty and friends joined them in prayer. When the project was presented to the several hundred guests attending the spring conference, enough money was given in offerings to cover the costs of one summer missionary. Dad took it as a definite signal that God wanted him to return to Germany.

Two months later, during the summer of 1950, he was on his way with almost one hundred other volunteers. Youth for Christ erected large tents for evangelistic meetings and hundreds crowded into them night after night as Dad preached in his less than fluent German.

Serving alongside Dad as song leader was Ellis Zehr. At several campaigns, they were assisted by Anton Schulte and Wilfried Zibell, who served as tent masters to the "foreign" evangelists. (Schulte would become one of Germany's most renowned evangelists, and Zibell was later an interpreter for Billy Graham in Germany.) Together, the friends shared unforgettable experiences.

In Karlsruhe-Durlach, the tent was pitched in an open area amid rubble and ruin from bombings. But it was so packed every night that many people were forced to stand outside. One evening, 60 people responded to the invitation to come forward and receive Jesus as Savior. Another night, 40 came forward. In the afternoons, the tent was filled with children who gathered for special meetings. One of their songs impacted Dad powerfully:

> *Jesus mein Heiland, Du hast mich lieb*
> *Die Bibel sagt es und sie trugt nicht.*
> *Wenn hier auf Erden auch alles bricht*
> *Bleibst Du mein Heiland und hast mich lieb.*

(Jesus, my Savior, you love me
The Bible says so and it does not lie.
When here on earth everything crumbles
You remain my Savior and love me so.)

That summer, Dad saw a war-ravaged country, demolished cities, and ruined houses. But he also met people with tender hearts, ready to hear God's Word and respond to Him with joy. The separation from family back in Canada had been hard on him and on Mother and us children. I was 4 years old and Mother became concerned when I lost my carefree spirit and grew listless—often I'd sit in the rocking chair with tears silently spilling down my cheeks. She called in the family doctor, who confirmed her suspicions: I was simply lonesome. Sure enough, Dad came home and my spirits lifted. All was right with the world again.

A few months later, Dad was planning to visit his parents 3,000 miles away in Saskatchewan, Canada. To avoid another painful separation, my parents decided to let me join Dad for the trip, which would include a train ride across the continent! (Children 5 years of age and younger were allowed to ride for free). I could hardly contain my excitement. To help prepare Dad for my personal care, Mother managed to teach him to braid my fine, straight hair; decorate the braids with ribbons; and even coax and gel a curl at each ear!

That trip was unforgettable—just me and my Dad. We watched the scenery whiz past, sang for the passengers in the dining car, and were lulled to sleep by the clickety-clack of the train on its track.

As little girls, my sister Sharon and I grew up singing. Dad accompanied us on guitar and soon we were singing in churches where Dad was invited to preach. At one Sunday evening service, the gospel message I had heard so often from Dad penetrated deeply into my heart. Sometimes when Dad preached, I would lie down on the front pew and sleep during the sermon until Dad would gently awaken me to sing a final song. Children can get away with that sort of thing! This night, however, I tuned in to the message Dad was giving. He described in vivid detail the unjust treatment of Jesus, His suffering in Gethsemane, and His agony on the cross of Calvary. Suddenly it all became clear: "Donna, Jesus suffered for *you*. Jesus died in *your* place. *You* should have suffered and died for your own sins, but Jesus died instead of YOU!"

The impact of it all was both shattering and redemptive to my young heart, and I started to cry. Dad, looking down, noticed my tears but didn't know what was wrong. Thinking I might be overtired or emotionally spent, he stopped preaching, walked down from the pulpit, and suggested I lie down on the pew and get some rest. He covered me carefully with his suit jacket and went back to finish his sermon. I am forever grateful that I heard about a loving heavenly Father from such a gracious earthly father.

NEW CHALLENGES

At an all-night prayer meeting at First Baptist Church in Downers Grove, Illinois, Dad's friend and song leader in Germany, Ellis Zehr, listened to a report on a recently established Bible institute in France. Speaker Noel Lyons, director of the Greater Europe Mission, said the organization needed someone to pioneer a similar training center in Germany. At a midnight break in the prayer meeting, Lyons invited Ellis Zehr outside for a walk to further discuss the project. "Ellis, we now have a building in Germany, which is a miracle in itself, but we need the right man to direct the work," Lyons said.

"I think I know the right man," Zehr responded. "John Parschauer."

A short time later, Dad received a letter from Lyons asking him to consider the venture. After several interviews and much prayer, the Greater Europe Mission invited our family to move to Germany and establish the school there.

Accepting the invitation meant Mom and we children would have to make some tremendous, difficult adjustments. We knew full well about the postwar conditions in Europe thanks to Dad's firsthand accounts of his past two summers there. Thousands were still living in underground refugee camps. Grocery stores were sparsely stocked. Businesses were struggling. Schools were disrupted. Railroads and highways were in disrepair. Cities were in ruins and housing was expensive.

Mom's perception of Germany had been shaped significantly by the horror stories of concentration camp victims and the demonic ravings of Hitler over the radio. She was faced with the decision: Should we leave our quiet, comfortable life in the peaceful country setting along the Saint John River to raise a family in a war-ravaged land? My parents were fulfilled in the thriving ministry of the Bible school and had developed deep friendships among the staff and faculty members. We children had close bonds with the other campus kids. My brother John was always racing bikes and wagons with his friends. Sharon and I could easily walk to the one-room schoolhouse just down the maple-lined road. Darlene was only two years old. But still, Mom and Dad knew they couldn't deny God's call.

In one of her journals, Mom wrote, "As softly as the first rays of early dawn pierce the darkness of the blackest night, even as softly came God's assurance and confirmation of His will." She also memorized a verse from a poem by George MacDonald that helped her through the difficult time of decision-making:

> I said, "But the sky is so dark
> There is nothing but noise and din!"
> And He wept as He sent me back,
> "There is more," He said
> "There is sin."
> I pleaded for time to be given.
> He said, "Is it hard to decide?
> It will not seem hard in heaven
> To have followed the steps of your Guide."

Finally, Dad and Mom agreed to accept the challenge of pioneering a Bible school in Germany. They agreed to stay at New Brunswick Bible Institute until student graduation in May 1954.

At the spring conference in May, the Bible school and the Canadian Sunday School Mission (CSSM) hosted a farewell service for our family. The director of CSSM, Walter Aikenhead and Noel Lyons, director of the Greater Europe Mission were on hand, and hundreds of friends offered financial support and prayer. The following day, we started out on deputation—a tour of churches across Canada to share the vision for missions in Germany.

Our tour was to begin in western Canada after visiting Grandma Matilda. She was critically ill, so we drove straight through to Saskatchewan to see her as soon as possible. Dad's father, Grandpa Henry, had died in February, and Grandma Matilda kept asking, "When is John coming?" Family members who knew we were on the way encouraged her to hold on until Dad got there, asking, "Don't you want to see John?" Her answer: "Yes, but I'd rather see Jesus." She died a few hours before we arrived.

At Grandma's funeral, Sharon and I sang the gospel song, "Where Could I Go but to the Lord," a fitting song for a woman who had made the Lord her refuge all her life. Standing beside her casket, I saw tears stream down my father's face as I sang the spiritual, "Precious Lord, Take My Hand":

Precious Lord, take my hand.
Lead me on, help me stand
I am tired, I am weak, I am worn
Through the storm, through the night
Lead me on to the Light
Take my hand, precious Lord, lead me home.
When my way grows drear,
Precious Lord, linger near
When my life is almost gone
Hear my cry, hear my call
Hold my hand lest I fall
Take my hand, precious Lord, lead me home.

DEPARTURE

The challenge of raising voyage expenses, four years' worth of financial support, and supplies for a family of six was daunting, but God did the impossible. In less than six months, we were ready to go. We counted down our final days in New Brunswick with the final chapel service, the last meals in the homes of our campus friends, the last hugs from Bible school students, and the last dinner at the home of "Uncle" Mark and "Auntie" Mildred Bredin.

At 6 p.m. on a November night, it was already dark as Ken and Ruth Robins packed the last of our suitcases into their car. They had offered to drive us the five hundred miles to the harbor in New York City. Dad and Mom knew the students were in the dining hall, and that we'd want to see them for one last goodbye before driving off for good. Dad and 5-year-old Johnnie went ahead and opened the door, while Mom, Sharon, Darlene, and I paused a moment to blink back tears.

It was so hard to leave all that was familiar and dear to us. Our campus friends had become like brothers and sisters to us. We played together in the snow, in piles of maple leaves, in each other's homes, along the Saint John River bank picking fiddleheads in the spring. We'd walked to school together, fought, and made up. And now it was over.

If it was wrenching for us children, I can only imagine how hard it must have been for Dad and Mom. They'd spent their entire married life in New Brunswick. Four healthy children had been born here. The student body had grown from 10 to 150. The facilities had evolved from a small, rented farm house to include a complete 20-acre campus of newly built structures as well as a children's camp on Davidson Lake, one of the loveliest lakes in the Maritimes. And they, too, were saying goodbye to precious friends: Ken and Ruth Robins, and Mark and Mildred Bredin. The strong bond they'd formed during years of friendship and ministry made leaving so hard but at the same time provided the strength Dad and Mom needed to embrace a new challenge.

CHAPTER 6
THE GREAT FAMILY ADVENTURE

Docked in the New York harbor, gleaming in the sun, the *SS United States* was an impressive sight. At nearly one thousand feet long, one hundred feet wide and weighing 53,300 gross tons, she was the largest and most luxurious ship built in America up to that time. She was also the fastest, setting new transatlantic speed records on her maiden voyage.

We children were awestruck and excited at the prospect of a new adventure, but we also sensed the grief and loss of what we were leaving behind. Dad and Mom were strong for our sakes as they hugged their precious friends Ken and Ruth Robins one final time before boarding.

On December 1, 1954, we watched silently from the ship's deck as the Statue of Liberty faded from view. We knew it would be four years before we would see our dear friends again.

The five-day voyage to Bremerhaven in northern Germany was smooth and pleasant. We kids loved the swimming pool and all of the on-deck activities. And we'd never eaten so well: fresh strawberries, steak, lobster. We weren't used to such sumptuous dining, and Darlene, who was 2, had particularly simple tastes. No matter what delicacies our server, a gracious African man named Samson, tried to tempt her with, Darlene always responded by saying, "No thanks. May I have corn flakes?"

When we docked in Bremerhaven, we were met by Kurt and Ruth Jung, and Rheinnie and Helen Barth. (Kurt and Rheinnie had been Youth for Christ team members with Dad in Europe four years earlier.) They drove us south to Bensheim on the Bergstrasse and helped us get temporarily settled into a villa on the edge of town. Our villa would become headquarters for the German Bible Institute.

Finding a facility for the Bible school had taken a miracle. Devastation from the war bombings had created a huge housing crisis. The government had confiscated every available building to meet the desperate needs of thousands of homeless refugees. Bob Evans, director of the Greater Europe Mission, had searched in vain for months. Traveling on the train one day, Evans met Paula Brandt, a former missionary to Turkey who was now retired and living in Switzerland. Evans shared with her the vision for a Bible school and the need for a suitable location.

As it turned out, Frau Brandt owned the stone villa in Bensheim. It had been occupied by the American Secret Service but was now standing empty. Furthermore, because Frau Brandt's deceased husband was from Denmark, the German government could not demand the use of her home. She gladly agreed to rent it to the Greater Europe Mission.

The villa would house our family as well as the first Bible school students. As we drove through the wrought iron gate at 29 Ernst Ludwigstrasse, the place looked like a mansion to us with its magnificent landscaping and huge, wraparound stone deck. The rooms were large and sunny, with shiny hardwood floors and a winding staircase leading up to the three rooms that would be our apartment. There was no furniture. Without beds, so we all had to sleep on mattresses on the floor. And there was no heat. The house had stood empty for quite a while and the furnace was stubbornly refusing to give up its warmth. After three days of coaxing and adjusting, it finally surrendered and began to pour out some very welcome heat.

In spite of these challenges, I don't remember ever hearing a word of complaint from Mom (who at the time was seven months pregnant with her fifth child). She knew that, in time, the Lord would provide. And she was right.

A man named Hugo Schneider, whom Dad had met during summer missions projects, offered to drive Dad in his truck to Frankfurt to do some Christmas shopping. (We didn't have a car of our own because cars were extremely scarce and expensive.) With Mr. Schneider's help, Dad was able to locate and buy new beds and mattresses, which arrived just in time for Christmas. We kids were delighted with our new beds, but Mom and Dad wanted to give us something else, something less functional and more fun. And so they sent us on a treasure hunt (I can still feel the excitement) until we found it: a brand new, two-wheeled scooter! Our parents opened the French doors and let us whiz across the hardwood floors throughout the spacious empty rooms, unhindered by either carpet or furniture.

Our Christmas tree was enormous. Dad bought the biggest one he could find and placed it in the middle of the living room. We decorated it according to German tradition: with real candles. Dad always did the grocery shopping for the family, partly because Mother didn't know the German language well and partly because Dad took delight in bringing God's provision home to us. He never took groceries for granted and would often display them on the counter so we could fully appreciate the bounty before storing it away. So Mother gave Dad her Christmas dinner shopping list: turkey, cranberries, sweet potatoes, and corn. This time, Dad came home defeated. "I don't know if it's them or me, but I can't find much on this list," he said. With her characteristic flexibility and positive spirit, Mom adapted her menu; and on Christmas day, we sat down to a delicious un-American feast.

After some games, Dad handed out sparklers and we waved them high as we circled the tree singing carols. My brother John declared it was "the best Christmas ever!" and we all agreed. Dad and Mother would later say they had felt literally carried by the sweet peace and presence of God and by the love and prayers of our dear friends across the ocean. As the evening drew to a close, we all gathered to read the Christmas story from Luke 2 and to pray. One by one we prayed, and when it was my turn, I started out strong, thanking God for the blessings of the day. But my voice quivered and trailed off as I added, "and bless the kids back home at the campus." My tears opened the floodgate for everyone else.

We were lonely, yes, but we also had many experiences during the month of December that gave us perspective and made our challenges seem comparatively small. One was our visit to the underground refugee camp in Mannheim. The residents there had lost everything during the war, and some of them had been living in the bunker since the war ended nine years earlier. To cheer them, Dad, Sharon, and I had been invited to sing the few songs we'd learned since coming to Germany.

Walking down the long flight of cement stairs, we came to a labyrinth of hallways, each dimly lit by a single bulb. Doorways punctuated the halls evenly, opening into small, cell-like cement rooms. As Dad began strumming his guitar, we girls started singing:

> Es gibt eine Heimat im himmlishen Licht
> Bereitet vom Heilande mein
> Und wenn Er mich heimruft so weiss ich gewiss
> Ich werde kein Fremdling dort sein.

> There is a home in the heavenly Light
> Prepared by my Savior
> And when He calls me home I know for sure
> That I'll be no stranger up there.

People began gathering in the doorways. People with care-worn faces listened with appreciation to our songs and to the encouraging words Dad spoke. Then we'd move along to the next central hub from which more hallways extended like spokes on a wheel. Again, Sharon and I sang our memorized songs, and again, Dad would share his personal testimony and some comfort from the Christmas story. We were approaching the final hub when our guide, the superintendent of the city mission, paused to caution us.

"The men in this hall are tough, bitter, and belligerent," he warned. "They may not accept your Christmas offerings."

But Dad encouraged us to continue, and we kept singing, our voices echoing down the empty hallway: "*Stille Nacht, heilige Nacht. Alles schlaeft, einsam wacht . . .*" As we were singing about "heavenly peace" and "Love's pure light," one by one the doors opened and men stood listening in silence—a silence that was hard to interpret. As we made our way to the exit, we heard feet shuffling behind us and turned to see a group of men approaching, their hands extended. We couldn't understand what they were saying, but we understood the tears in their eyes as they handed us gifts: a few coins, an orange, some candies. Back in New Brunswick we had sung at music festivals where there were accolades and awards, but nothing ever compared to the rich reward we felt that night singing hope into darkness.

ADJUSTMENTS

We had no orientation classes to prepare us for life in another culture. But God sent help through neighbors and friends of Frau Brandt. The caretakers of our villa, the Kuntz's, had four grown daughters who were always ready to help in any way they could. They knew how to coax our temperamental furnace into working. They helped Dad and Mom with foreign registration paperwork and later, when the Bible school opened, two of the sisters helped cook for the first conference. Two who were kindergarten teachers tutored us kids.

Dad did his best to help us learn the German language by giving us a few new words each day and teaching us the phonetic pronunciation of song lyrics. Often, we didn't understand exactly what we were singing!

But the greatest help came from attending German schools. Many of the school buildings were not yet rebuilt or restored, so we rotated—attending the "cold" school one day, and the school without desks another. That way, all students shared the disadvantages equally. The German children were friendly and anxious to help us strange foreigners. During recess one day, a girl came toward me brandishing a big stick. I was terrified until I realized what she was doing. She pointed to the stick and repeated "Stock. Stock. Stock," giving me my new word for the day.

Mom struggled with war-related fears and was very watchful of our safety. She made our brother John check in every 15 minutes when he was outside playing. Johnnie would run into the house every quarter hour, giving Mom proof he was safe and sound, and then run off for another 15 minutes. That winter, when Dad was away on speaking engagements, our English-speaking neighbor Liese Haarhaus stayed with us and helped Mother in the last stages of pregnancy.

Johnnie, who was 6 and outnumbered three to one by us girls, was hoping and praying for a baby brother. One day, his faith faltering, he confided tearfully to Mom, "I just *know* the girls are going to laugh at me if our baby is a girl!" Mother reassured him and every night he prayed, "Help that our baby will be the biggest in the hospital." Mom asked him why, and he explained, "So he'll grow up fast so I can play with him." On Valentine's Day, 1955, baby Kennie was born in Mannheim hospital. When the nurse brought him in to Mom, she announced, "I've just weighed all the babies in the nursery, and yours is the biggest in the whole hospital!"

In March, Pastor Fussle, whose family had so miraculously survived the 1944 Freiburg air raid, invited Dad to a week of meetings in Stuttgart. Sharon and I sang at each service, and the rest of the family joined us for the weekend. It was a privilege to stay in the Fussle home and get to know the family. Our families became close friends, and as young adults, three of the six Fussle children attended the Bible school.

Two months later, Dad led a two-week evangelistic tent crusade sponsored by Youth for Christ in Duisburg. Helen Barth was soloist, and Sharon and I learned new German songs to sing for each meeting. Ruth Frey, a renowned children's speaker, led special services for children in the afternoon, and many of them trusted Jesus as Savior. Some of them even went on to attend the Bible school.

While in Duisburg, we stayed with Wilhelm Schrooten and his family. While we were there, Mom asked about a picture of a little boy on the piano, and Mrs. Schrooten proceeded to tell us the most amazing story. The child was her oldest son, who had died of leukemia at age four. The boy was diagnosed with the disease while his father was in the army during the war. As a result, he knew nothing of his child's illness and was not expected to receive leave any time soon. During nightly air raids, Mrs. Schrooten would gather the boy in her arms and rush him to the crowded, damp bomb shelter. Almost delirious one evening, he kept calling out for his Papa. A tender heavenly Father was listening and that very night, Mr. Schrooten walked into the house unannounced having received an unexpected leave of absence. He made it home in time to hold his son as he passed away.

The gracious hospitality of families like the Fussles and the Schrootens made us feel welcome and accepted in a war-torn country. Fear and prejudice toward "Germans" gave way to lasting friendships with people who had endured sorrow and loss, who had been sustained by God, and whose faith and compassion touched us deeply.

CHAPTER 7
GERMAN BIBLE SCHOOL GROWS... AND GROWS

As God brought students to study the Scriptures, He also built a staff to work in unity of heart and purpose. First to join the team was Ernie Klassen, who had served as staff evangelist at New Brunswick Bible Institute. Ernie was raised on a Saskatchewan prairie farm by strict German Mennonite parents. As a teenager, Ernie had little interest in spiritual things, until a friend arrived one Sunday with tragic news. Ernie's older brother, Dave, had drowned trying to get his cattle across the swollen river. The sudden loss brought young Ernie face to face with eternal issues: the brevity of life and God's ultimate purpose for it. He committed his heart to the Lord and enrolled in Millar Memorial Bible Institute, the same school Dad attended in Pambrun.

Ernie served in the Royal Canadian Air Force and after the war traveled throughout Germany as an interpreter, forming many personal relationships. In 1950, he was a teacher at New Brunswick Bible Institute. When Dad returned from his mission trip that summer with reports of the spiritual needs in Germany, Ernie sensed God's call on his heart. In 1955, Ernie, his wife Erma, and their three children joined us in Germany.

When they arrived, preparations were well underway for the first school term, which would begin in the fall. In a letter to friends in Chicago, Dad wrote:

> So much needs to be done before school starts. A secretary is sorely needed; the office work has us snowed under! The orchard on our property requires an enormous amount of attention. The Lord undertook for this pressing need by sending us a layman gardener for two weeks. Maureen has canned 80 quarts of cherries and 20 quarts of strawberries. Much more fruit needs to be picked! We had 73 overnight

guests this past month and we served 450 meals apart from our own family meals! All our guests were vitally interested in the Bible school.

Swiss-born Heinz Weber joined the staff as a remarkably gifted Bible and theology teacher. Raised by a godly aunt, Heinz, at age 16, made a decision to accept Christ as Savior, but for five or six years, he resisted God's call on his life. He wanted to taste the pleasures of the world and do his own thing. In his rebellion, he resented the prayers and counsel of his aunt. But God kept pursuing Heinz's heart. When Heinz finally surrendered, he transferred from college to attend Beatenberg Bible School, where he received excellent training, both academic and spiritual. He made plans to go to Africa as a missionary after graduation but health issues prevented him from going. And so in coming to Bensheim, he found fulfillment training others for the ministry, both in Germany and around the world. He and Dad became close friends, always treating each other with respect.

Thirteen young students made up the first class. Dr. Carl Armerding of Wheaton College spoke at the opening conference on October 7, 1955. The next year there were 28 students. The third year, 54. During the summer months, staff and students took part in evangelistic campaigns and camps. The camps were held at the Bible school villa. Forty-one children attended the first one, followed by a 10-day teen camp. The third camp was for English-speaking German youth. For many, it was the first time they'd heard the gospel, and many trusted Christ and gave their testimonies on closing night.

Another wonderful addition to the mission team staff was Barbara MacLeod, a teacher from Nova Scotia, Canada and a graduate of New Brunswick Bible Institute, where we had grown to know and love her. Dad and Mom had invited her to come over to Germany to teach us and the other staff children. I had added my own crookedly handwritten letter of invitation and was sure my plea had convinced Barbara or "Auntie Barb," as we called her, to join us in Germany. Auntie Barb became far more than a teacher to us; I remember nestling beside her on the sofa as she introduced me to the wonders of *Winnie the Pooh*, *Anne of Green Gables*, and other children's classics. Auntie Barb was always

German Bible School Grows... and Grows 49

game for a slumber party or a tea party or making fudge or her famous lemon pudding. She never forgot a birthday and was notorious for her generosity. Later, when we all were fluent in German and could again attend German schools, Barbara became the dean of women at the Bible school, nurturing and mentoring scores of students. She never married and the reason for it she gave in her famous line, "I never met a man who deserved to be as happy as I could make him!" She spent her life giving to the spiritual children God entrusted to her around the world.

After two years, the Bible school had outgrown the villa. A rundown hotel nearby—Hotel Weigold in Auerbach—was rented for additional classroom space. It had stood empty for three years, so it needed intensive cleaning; the dirt layers were so thick as to completely hide the hardwood floors. Every morning, the students would have to make the half-hour walk from their dorm rooms in the original villa in Bensheim to their classrooms in the hotel. The leadership team knew they would have to pray for another location.

Again, God provided. A few miles away in Seeheim, a magnificently landscaped old castle was found vacant and for sale for 100,000 German marks. Already financially stretched, the Bible school had no fund from which to draw resources . . . except God. Within several months, supporters on both sides of the ocean had sent in the needed amount! The campus was dedicated at the spring conference in May 1958, with a thousand people gathered on the lawn to witness the graduation of the first Bible school students. Each of the graduates went on to full-time ministry, some staying in Germany as church and parachurch workers and others going out as missionaries to other countries. The student body enrollment was now up to 70. God was at work in a powerful way, preparing dedicated workers in the Kingdom of God. Years later, one of the graduates, evangelist Willi Buchwald, wrote about the influence that the Bible school teachers had made in his life and 35-year ministry. Of Dad he said,

> Brother Parschauer and his family lived with us students in the "Brandt" villa. We had and needed strict rules, but we were a happy lot! Mr. Parschauer with his humor contributed much

to that atmosphere. In his love and wholeheartedness, he was not only director but father to us. His seriousness about the Word of God and his personal witness to others have left a deep impact on me.

Ministry for Dad and Mom often moved beyond the borders of the Bible School. Bensheim was only about a 20-minute drive from Benjamin Franklin Village, an American army base near Darmstadt. Dad and Mother soon made some connections with people there and before too long, they were asked to teach junior church at the Chapel on base. When they started, about 35 children attended. The numbers grew until almost two hundred children filled the auditorium on the lower level of the church while the adult worship service was going on upstairs. It was quite a challenge to get the attention of a group that large at the beginning of junior church, until Dad came up with an idea. He produced a stick pin from his lapel and then told the kids to listen to see if they could hear the pin drop. The noise level in the room dropped to absolute silence as they all strained to hear the tiny sound. Each Sunday from then on, Dad would signal the start of the service by his upraised hand holding the pin! Both Dad and Mother were captivating story tellers and used "flannelgraph" and creative objects to teach Bible truth. We kids helped with leading the music. Quite a few children came to trust Jesus as Savior, and years later, some of them contacted Dad and Mother to thank them . . . and each of them remembered the "pin drop"!

One particular out-of-town experience during those years in Europe stands out in my mind. The occasion was the inauguration of the Canadian War Memorial in Holland in 1958. Dad and Mother had been asked to represent the parents of a young man, Charles Fuller who had fallen in battle during World War II and who had a special connection to Dad. Mother wrote a moving description of the day:

Our Visit to Canada's War Memorial in Holland

The first streaks of dawn had cast a rosy glow over the summer sky, when we awoke on the morning of June the 2nd. The day held promise of beauty.

German Bible School Grows... and Grows 51

We were glad, for this was the day of the unveiling of the Canadian War Memorial at Groesbeek, Holland. As we stood for a moment peering into the serene tints of the silent dawn, our hearts thrilled as the verse came to our minds, "This is the day which the Lord has made."

The trip of several hours was indeed beautiful. Europe is at its loveliest now. The many shades of spring's greens make a rich background for the gorgeous flowering shrubs and trees.

At the little village of Groesbeek, we stopped to ask an old gentleman crossing the street if he could tell us where the cemetery was located. At the mention of the Canadian War Memorial, he reverently removed his hat before giving us the directions. As we came over the hill, we could see the Canadian flag waving high on the knoll on which the cemetery is located. How good that flag looked to us! The roadside was lined for almost a half mile with Dutch schoolchildren and hundreds of Dutch people who hold the memory of our Canadian soldiers in high esteem.

Passing into the parent's enclosure inside the cemetery, I read the inscription carved into the frieze above the columns, "We live in the hearts of friends for whom we died." I recalled not only the dear ones across the Atlantic, but the old gentleman with his hat in hand, the rows of Dutch children and their parents and friends. Yes, they live in the hearts of these as well.

There were approximately 800 gathered within the reserved "parents" enclosure. They were surrounded by the Royal guards of Honor of the Canadian, British, and Dutch armies. The Royal Canadian Corps of Signals played appropriate selections of music. We felt honored to be representing A.C. Fuller of Earl Grey, Saskatchewan, whose son, Charles, is buried at Groesbeek. Charlie had been one of the students John had taught at Briercrest Bible Institute in Saskatchewan before the war started. His life had been characterized by integrity and strong spiritual commitment. John used to borrow Charlie's guitar sometimes when he was asked to sing in evangelistic meetings. After John moved to work in New Brunswick in 1944, he was surprised one day to get a package from Charlie. In it he found Charlie's own guitar accompanied with a short note: "I am going overseas to join the army, so I'm sending you my guitar. Chances are that I may not need it again. Use it for the glory of God . . . ."

Presently, the royal limousines arrived. The British and Netherlands national anthems were played as the Duke of Gloucester and the Prince of the Netherlands entered and received royal salutes. We thought it was fitting that

Prince Bernard could be present, since his wife (now queen of the Netherlands) and three daughters had found refuge in Canada during the war, as guests of Queen Juliana's Aunt Alice and her husband, then Governor General, the Earl of Athlone.

It was impressive to then hear the many voices blended in the well-loved hymn "O God Our Help in Ages Past"...some singing in Dutch, some in English. The Duke of Gloucester gave an address, speaking with tenderness and compassion . . . a noble tribute to those in whose memory we were gathered. The actual unveiling of the memorial followed.

Beside me stood a freckled red-haired lad of about 12 or 14 bravely trying to comfort his mother as they bowed before his Dad's gravestone engraved with the words, "To the world a soldier; to us the world."

After the ceremony, we looked up Charlie's grave. John took out Charlie's guitar, and in tribute to him and his Lord, accompanied Sharon and Donna as they stood behind Charlie's gravestone and sang a short chorus:

> Just a little longer and the trump of God shall sound
> Just a little longer and we'll all be glory bound
> Look away to heaven, your redemption draweth nigh
> Just a little longer and we'll meet Him in the sky.

We were among the last to leave the Groesbeek Memorial that day. As we turned to go, a lovely European skylark rose from among the grave stones. It soared into the heavens, singing and soaring, singing and soaring. It reminded me of Shelley's poem, "To a Skylark." This was my first time to see and hear one. It seemed appropriate that the beautiful song of this heavenly minstrel should be the finale to the memorial service. Though loved ones had to go, God's little songster remained, singing a benediction from the heavens over this sacred spot.

"In the morning and at the going down of the sun, we shall remember them."

Maureen Parschauer, June 1958

ON THE ROAD AGAIN: 1958 "FURLOUGH"

Four years had gone by, and it was time for our family to go back to Canada on furlough. Aboard the ship, 3-year-old Kennie had bouts of seasickness and kept complaining that "this old house keeps going up and down!"

It was early dawn when we approached New York Harbor. Mother woke us early to catch the first glimpse of the Statue of Liberty shrouded in morning mist. A moving sight! After a wonderful reunion with our old friends in New Brunswick, we spent the summer traveling across the country in a station wagon, pulling a 17-foot trailer to visit friends, family, and supporting churches. There was a church service almost every night. Dad would give a report and show his slides, and Sharon and I would sing.

Mom and Dad tried to make the trip as interesting as possible, finding scenic points along the way. We'd stop to play hide and seek and borrow stacks of book to read. We'd stop at picnic areas and help Mom prepare lunch in the trailer. A grocer we'd met at one of the church services gave us a box of "slightly damaged" canned goods, some without their identifying labels. For lunch one day, Mom opened an unmarked can and found something . . . nondescript. "This must be the 'bully beef' the grocer told me about," she figured. It looked dry, so she mixed it with some soup and tried to make it look more appetizing by topping off each bowl with a dollop of French's mustard. We kids had always been taught not to complain about food that was served to us, but Dad could see we were clearly having trouble with this. My father, who would eat *anything* without complaining, took a generous spoonful of the "bully beef" and flung it into a nearby bush! All five of us followed his lead, gleefully and with great abandon sending bully-beef missiles into the bushes. When Mom peered out of the doorway, we gladly reported that "Daddy started it!" It was the first and last time she served us bully beef, which she later found out was dog food!

Dad always brought his sense of humor to the families who hosted us. He would connect with the little children with a snapping of his fingers over his knuckles and a beeping of their noses. And he would compliment the hostess on the "malicious deal!" We chuckled at the jokes that we heard over and over. We liked having a dad who was fun and who didn't take himself too seriously.

CHAPTER 8
GOD'S WAY UP IS DOWN

We returned to Germany the next year, in July 1959. While we had been in the states on "furlough," disagreement arose between the newly assigned Greater Europe Mission teachers at the school and the original team over the direction and vision of the Bible school. Greater Europe Mission wanted to move the school toward seminary accreditation geared toward the training of primarily national pastors. Ernie Klassen and Heinz Weber shared Dad's vision for biblical teaching that included a strong missionary emphasis. Now that emphasis on missions that was so close to their hearts seemed to be threatened. Instead of resisting the new direction of the mission, the three leaders chose to leave the school. Dad resigned from the Greater Europe Mission.

I can only imagine the heartache that surrounded that decision, which must have seemed like a death of some kind, but I can't recall any bitterness spilling from Dad that contaminated the atmosphere in our home. Some of the students urged Dad to start again . . . pioneer another school consistent with the original vision. But was that the right thing to do? Would it be reactive or competitive in spirit? Was there room for another Bible school in Germany? After much prayer and discussion with German church leaders, Dad was encouraged to found another school under the newly formed German Missionary Fellowship. To minimize misunderstanding, the three teachers took nothing material or financial when they left. Only a simple faith in a God who directs and provides. The Bible school in Seeheim (now located in Konigsfeld) developed into a school recognized in Germany for faithful Bible education. And today, there is a harmonious brotherly relationship between the two schools.

ASKING FOR MIRACLES

Plans were made to open a new school that very fall in 1959. Ernie and Heinz had a facility in mind, a former private school owned by the city of Hennef. All that stood in the way was permission from the

Hennef city council to lease the property. When the council convened that August and was told what the property would be used for, their answer was "No."

Dad had announced the opening date for the new Bible school as October 1, 1959, but the search for property was getting desperate. Real estate agents and lawyers scoffed at the impossibility of the challenge. "You mean you want to find a place to house 30 students in less than a month?" they asked. "It would take longer than that to get the paperwork done. You might be able to find something that fast in America but not here in Germany!" Nevertheless, 30 students had already been accepted, and Dad sent a letter assuring them and their families that they would hear soon where the school would be located.

On September 1, Dad was driving through Duisburg and stopped to visit Mrs. Schrooten, who had trusted Christ as Savior at a tent meeting where Dad preached during his summer ministry with Youth for Christ in 1950. Dad told Mrs. Schrooten about the urgent need for a Bible school facility.

"Last week, I visited my sister at Kalkar. She spoke of a vacant 32-room hotel/villa close by," Mrs. Schrooten said. Kalkar was about an hour's drive away, in northwest Germany near the Holland border. Dad, Ernie, and Heinz drove there immediately to check out the villa called Haus Horst. They followed a long, shady tree-lined lane up to big iron gates that opened into a large, gracious villa surrounded by a moat!

The owner, Mr. Eichoff, just happened to be there when the men drove up the circular drive. He was willing to lease the property for three years, with the stipulation that one year's rent be paid in advance. The former occupants had failed to make their payments, and Mr. Eichoff was determined to get his money this time. The annual rent was a seemingly astronomical 12,000 DM (approximately $3,000). In spite of his sticker shock, Dad told Mr. Eichoff he and the search team would pray about it and give him an answer as soon as possible. The place seemed ideal, but coming up with the money seemed impossible. Trusting God for a miracle yet again, Dad and his colleagues started praying.

Within the week, a letter arrived from the father of a prospective student. Mr. Willnat's daughter had received Christ as Savior at one of Dad's meetings in Duisburg and was now planning to attend Bible school. In gratitude, Mr. and Mrs. Willnat enclosed a check for 7,500 DM (almost $2,000), the largest contribution ever made to the Bible school ministry. Soon after, the full amount needed to pay the first year's rent was raised, and those who had been praying celebrated God's amazing provision by packing up for the move to Kalkar.

There were still some staffing needs to be met, including finding a cook. A woman had been hired for the position, but at the last minute she had to cancel, leaving an opening that became urgent to fill. Just before Dad left to investigate the Kalkar site, a young woman, Gerda Burkert, came to offer to help in the kitchen. Gerda's own life journey had been a difficult one. As an only child, she and her mother had fled East Germany as Russian troops advanced into their homeland. Fatherless and homeless, Gerda and her mother found refuge in western Germany with her elderly grandmother. She had a strong faith in Jesus Christ and wanted to give her life for Him. She was not a trained chef and had no intention of taking on the full responsibilities in the kitchen, but she came with a willing heart to serve God. With some persuasion, she agreed to take on the position of chef in total dependence on God. Gerda became, in Dad's words, "a godsend to us." Her service at the new Bible school was an answer to much fervent prayer. From her primitive but spotless kitchen, Gerda served wonderful meals with a joyful spirit that would nourish the students, staff, and thousands of guests over the next 25 years.

In answer to the Bible school's need for an administrative secretary, God brought Irmgard Willnat, a young woman proficient in both German and English. As a child, Irmgard had also known the terrors of war. When French soldiers barged into her family's house, Irmgard lay sick in bed. A soldier asked if she was ill, and Irmgard held her breath, closed her eyes, and didn't move a muscle as her mother answered yes. She expected the worst, but instead the soldiers left. Their lives had been spared.

As a teenager, Irmgard received an offer to work in Toronto, Ontario primarily to learn English. While there, she attended the

People's Church, where God deepened her spiritual life and ignited a vision for missions. When she returned to Germany and heard of some Canadians starting a Bible school that emphasized missions, Irmgard accepted the job as Dad's administrative secretary until she became the lovely bride of Heinz Weber in 1960.

The pieces of the puzzle were being placed together by a divine hand. The staff was forming, students were enrolled, and the property was leased. Yet with classes set to begin in less than a month, the buildings were still completely unfurnished. A good used stove was purchased along with dishes, tables, chairs, cupboards, and kitchen utensils. The very week that the bill arrived for almost 8,000 DM, another check arrived for 7,500 DM, this time from a businesswoman who owned a large printing company.

Mr. Eichoff asked for a substantial sum to rent the drapes for the villa. Dad said he'd never heard of paying rent on curtains in his life! Someone told him of a drapery factory near Heidelberg. So he made an appointment with the company president, a Christian businessman. After Dad explained the mission, the president decided to donate custom-made drapes and curtains for all 32 rooms in the building!

Finding beds was another challenge. Typical German beds were too large. Dutch beds were too expensive. Army beds were suitable but rarely available. Ernie Klassen drove to Wiesbaden to ask a Colonel Ferguson if any army beds were available. The colonel said beds were almost impossible to get but asked how many were needed. "About 50," Ernie answered. Colonel Ferguson checked and called with news that there were exactly 50 beds for sale! He bought them personally, along with the mattresses, and donated them to the Bible school.

The beds had to be transported two hundred miles from Wiesbaden to Kalkar. While discussing how to get them there, Herr Schrooten, who owned a transport company, happened to call. When he was told about the beds, he said, "Oh that's not a problem. I'm driving with a loaded truck to Kaiserslautern and driving back empty. I'd be glad to stop in Wiesbaden and bring them to you." The beds arrived on the last day of September, the day before the students arrived! The 42 students, eager to study God's Word, didn't realize how close they had come to camping on the floor!

One of the students was Wilhelm Vichel, a refugee from East Germany who arrived unannounced. He had escaped from the east zone by swimming across the Elbe River. The border guards shot at him but Wilhelm believed that they purposely missed him because they knew him. At first, the leadership didn't know what to do with him because he hadn't sent in an application. They even wondered if he could be a spy! He had no money. But Wilhelm proved to be full of integrity and spiritual energy. He was a hard worker, always looking for practical ways to help and serve. A gardener by trade, he later did all the landscaping for the new property. After graduating, he and his wife Helene worked in Brazil as missionaries.

The theme verse for the new "Bible and Missions School" in Kalkar was 2 Timothy 2:2 (NIV): "The things you have heard me say in the presence of many witnesses, entrust to reliable men who will also be qualified to teach others." The motto served to underline for both teachers and students the principle of spiritual multiplication. What we learn we should entrust to others and so build the Kingdom of God.

LIFE IN HAUS HORST

Our family lived in a three-room apartment on the second floor of the Bible school villa. Sharon and I shared a bedroom. John, Darlene, and Ken slept on the living room sofas. The dining table was on the other side of the same room, so when we had guests, bedtime had to wait until the guests left. Dad and Mother partitioned off the kitchen to make a bedroom area for themselves. Somehow, I didn't give much thought to the fact that Dad and Mother had given Sharon and me the best bedroom. They never acted like they were sacrificing for us.

In the spring, our bedroom windows let in the fragrance of the lilacs blooming below us. Not quite as romantic was the plague of mice that we had to contend with in the same room! Most every night, Mother set four mouse traps in our room and our sleep was intermittently disturbed by the "clap!" of the trap and the dance of the dying mouse. To protect our sensibilities, Mother would come to our room early to dispose of the poor creatures before we woke. One winter, more than three hundred mice met their doom in our bedroom alone!

Close quarters didn't keep Dad and Mother from hosting scores of dinner guests. Mother taught us by example the difference between entertaining and "hospitality." She never entertained to show off her culinary or decorating skills or to look like "the perfect hostess." For her, hospitality was about people . . . making them feel loved and appreciated. If someone dropped by unannounced, she welcomed them warmly, even if the house wasn't in perfect order. Mother wasn't the greatest cook, but she had a few failsafe meals she could prepare at very short notice. A favorite dessert was "Whacky Cake," a chocolate cake that didn't call for either eggs or milk, so she usually had the necessary ingredients on hand. If Dad called Mom to give a head's up about guests who were soon to arrive, Mom would kick into action, get the Whacky Cake in the oven and beat up some whipping cream to top it off. If she had no time to bake something fresh, she had an amazing ability to take whatever she happened to have on hand, cover it with freshly whipped cream, and serve it with confidence. We girls weren't always quite as confident about the quality of the offering, but Mother believed that anything served on Royal Albert or Rosenthal china by candlelight was a sure success. "No one will complain about the food if the presentation is beautiful!"

I remember the laughter and fun of mealtimes with new guests and long-time friends, especially other missionary families. We loved being included in hilarious Rook games after dinner. Mom used to help us cheat by slipping us the card we needed. Dad would bid ridiculously high, hoping for a miraculous "kitty" or quipping, "I'm counting on my partner!"

Sharon and I attended an all-girls high school ("Gymnasium") in Kleve, 10 miles away. We either rode the bus or biked to school on one of the wide bike trails common in the flatlands there so near Holland. We were the only Canadian students, and the German girls and teachers made us feel very welcome. Everyone was required to take English, French, and Latin, so we managed to excel in at least one class!

John biked nine miles to an all-boys school in Goch. Some days he arrived home after school beet-red, drenched in sweat from trying to best his own personal record. Darlene, our sparkly little blond, blended in perfectly with the German children in the elementary school in Kalkar. Mother taught 4-year-old Kenny at home. He had a lot of contact with the Bible school students and some of them liked to practice their English on him. Once, in his typically gentle way, he said, "Mommy, you don't talk German quite right."

"Oh, really?" Mom answered. "How is that?"

"Well, you talk German like the students talk English to me!"

Sometimes, when the Bible school students were away on break, Dad and Mom let us invite our whole class home. Dad planned relay races, dodge ball, and volleyball games, and Mom made mounds of food. The girls loved it! They were surprised that the director of a Bible school could be so much fun and some walls of suspicion about a "cult" at Haus Horst were broken down as we built friendships with the love of Christ.

RADIO, RECORDINGS, AND MORE

Dad believed that the Great Commission of Jesus to "go into all the world" with the gospel needed to be emphasized; he prayed that missionary zeal be rekindled in Germany. With that focus, in 1961, he produced and directed "Ruf in den Weinberg" (The Vineyard Call), a 15-minute weekly radio broadcast that aired at 6:55 a.m. over Radio Luxembourg. With the linguistic help of some European students at the Bible school, Sharon and I had recorded songs in five languages which played on the program along with Dad's messages. The theme song for the program, "Gehe in den Weinberg" (Go into the Vineyard) was the very first German song that Dad taught Sharon and me, and God used it to challenge many to consider missions. Recordings by the "Parschauer Schwestern" became popular in Germany during that time.

During the weekends and summer months, the students were involved in mission outreaches or church ministries, putting their classroom training into practice. Twice a year, the conferences at the Bible school featured renowned guest preachers and drew hundreds of guests. Even if we kids missed a service and stayed home, the wonderful worship singing rose to fill our upstairs apartment!

"Haus Horst" was kept humming all year long. A thriving summer camp ministry brought whole families together for their vacation time. Other weeks were designed for children or teens only, and some of the students stayed through the summer as workers and counselors.

In 1960, 52 students from Germany, Switzerland, France, and Holland attended the Bible school. By that point, the hotel had been outgrown and the 3-year lease was almost up, so the school's leaders had to decide where to go next. Construction in congested Europe was complicated and fraught with legalities. Support teams in Germany and America joined the staff in praying for God's direction. And God began showing the way, step by miraculous step.

CHAPTER 9
GOD-SIZED CHALLENGES

At the fall conference that year, Dad spoke about needing a larger facility. With his typical dry wit, he half-joked, "If anyone has a property you want to give to us, we'll gladly accept it as from the Lord!" After the service, Frau Bunte, a widow who had come to the conference to witness the graduation of her daughter, approached Dad and said, "You're not going to believe this, but on the way here, I talked to my children about the possibility of offering our property to the Bible school. They are in full agreement. If you can use it, it's yours." Her property, 8,500 square meters of picturesque land, was in Brake, right next to the charming town of Lemgo, near Bielefeld. In 1905, Frau Bunte's father had planted an orchard on the property and the life motto of her parents had been "Bete und Arbeite" (pray and work). They likely never dreamed that their orchard would reap such a rich spiritual harvest years later!

Frau Bunte's offer was accepted with much thanksgiving. Her brother, Herr Wettlaufer, donated an adjacent smaller property.

Although it was common for building proposals in that part of Germany to take two years for approval, the school got permission to build in just two and a half weeks, and building plans were approved without any adjustments. A young Christian architect drew blueprints free of charge and pledged monthly support besides! Two other men donated their time to survey the land and they too pledged monthly support.

Herr Friedrich, a Christian builder from Stuttgart and the father of one of the school's graduates, took a leave of absence from his job to oversee construction, offering his services free of charge.

But what about excavation?

On a divine impulse, Dad went to the Canadian army base near Brake. Not knowing where to start, he went to the Chaplain who said he would request a two-minute appointment with the general. The request was denied, so Dad sat in his car in front of the office and put the appeal in writing. In the letter, he spoke about his vision and commitment to give back the Bible school to German young people. Finally, five weeks later, a Canadian army major came with the news: yes. The army has decided the Bible school was a worthy cause and offered its support.

"Would you be able to put the men up while they're working?" the major asked.

"Of course," Dad answered, even though there were no accommodations for the men. "That's the least we can do!"

The commander must have sensed some uncertainty and said, "Look, if it's a problem, just say so; we can send tents for the men to sleep in, and besides that, we'll send a cook to take care of all the meals for the men."

And so it was that an army of strong young Canadian soldiers arrived to help build the Bible school. The major had calculated that the job should take about 10 days. But because of rain, the bulldozers bogged down in the mud, extending the work time to a full month. But while it rained, the soldiers hauled in building blocks, bricks, and gravel. Through it all, a mighty God was in charge and His name was praised!

Dad heard of a contractor in Remscheid and made an appointment to explain the vision of the work to him. Dad was nervous about meeting Mr. Adolf Runkel. But the distinguished businessman quickly put him at ease. He listened attentively as Dad recounted the school's history and shared his vision for training young people for ministry in Europe and around the world. Before long, Dad was describing the projected building plans and showing Mr. Runkel the blueprints for a two-story building, 125 feet long, with adjoining kitchen and dining room, large enough to house 75 students and several staff families.

Finally, the question that Dad feared came: "How much capital do you have for this project?"

Dad coughed. "Frankly, Mr. Runkel, we have nothing."

To Dad's amazement Runkel answered, "Well, *then* I'm interested; then God can do something!" And for the next hour, he kept Dad spellbound with stories of his own experiences with faith projects where God had worked in incredible ways. At the end of their meeting, Mr. Runkel asked for a set of the blueprints.

"I can't promise anything, but I'll pray about how we can help."

Before they parted, Dad and Mr. Runkel knelt down together and prayed for God's direction in the project.

Not too long afterward, two huge trucks ground their way up to the construction site loaded with steel pre-bent according to the blueprints' exact specifications. Wheelbarrows, lumber, nails, hammers, saws, and more—Mr. Runkel sent everything except a bill. (Not long afterward, Mr. Runkel participated in the dedication of a new church he had helped build. From the podium, he encouraged the congregation and its pastoral staff with a call to faithfulness and integrity. In a moving ceremony, he handed the church keys to the pastor, sat down in the front row, and died suddenly. Thousands of people attended Mr. Runkel's funeral, a testimony to the impact of one man totally committed to the Kingdom of God.)

With only $150 in the bank and the excavation complete, construction began in the fall of 1961. Frau Bunte housed some of the workers in her home. Franz Friedrich, the contractor, suggested that it would be possible to erect the entire building with the volunteer help of students working under his supervision. Six of them interrupted their Bible school education for a year to work on the project.

Construction was an almost overwhelming challenge with no electricity or running water. Water had to be hauled from a brook nearby. Mr. Friedrich wasted nothing. Used nails were hammered straight and used again! It was an adventure for everybody as God gave energy and supplied daily needs. As the bills arrived, so did the money to pay for them. Donations and contributions covered the expenses and no money was borrowed. Most of the giving came from Germans; some even came from the students themselves. Significant donations came from German businessmen. Ernie Klassen was in the process of ordering a deep freeze and four automatic water heaters and phoned a Christian businessman about getting the units wholesale. In broken English the man said, "The wholesalers are doing anything and I am doing anything too." And the water heaters arrived as his gift to the Bible school.

Engineers and experts estimated that it would take at least five years to build a road and provide electricity, sewer systems, and water for the school. Everything was in place within eight months.

Nearly finished, the Bible school in Brake opened October 1, 1962. The classrooms were bare and uncarpeted but clean and painted. The ground was drenched from all the rain, so workers laid planks over the mud at the entrances to the building. Seventy students arrived with a spirit of adventure and a willingness to work. A remarkable spirit of deep unity among staff and students reigned where frustration could have festered over the primitive conditions and unfinished buildings.

The Bible school rented a 700-seat tent for the dedication ceremony at the fall conference, and even that was too small for the overflow of guests and friends who came to celebrate God's faithfulness. Every room in the new building was occupied and every bill was paid! To God be the glory!

The "Bibelschule" administrators knew Frau Bunte's property was too small for planned future expansion and prayed that surrounding land would become available. At first, none of the three property owners wanted to sell. But suddenly, for no apparent reason other than God, all three changed their minds and offered to sell their land to the school. Dad announced the miracle at the conference, and several generous people contributed enough to nearly cover the cost of the added properties.

In a newsletter he wrote on October 29, 1962, Dad told supporting friends in Canada and the United States, "I feel confident that many of these miracles have taken place because you prayed. We want to thank you from our hearts for your part in this work and for your faithfulness. He will surely reward you. Our heart's desire is that we may not only experience the miracle-working power of God in things financial and material but above all in things spiritual. May our school always be a Christ-centered, Bible-centered and missionary-centered training center."

SOMMERSELL

When we children learned we'd be moving away from Kalkar, naturally we wondered where our family would live. There wasn't room in the Bible school dormitory, and private rental homes were almost impossible to find or afford.

Still, 10-year-old Darlene came to Mother and asked if she might be able to have a room of her own when we moved. Sharing the living room with her two brothers was getting a little old.

"Well, maybe you and the dog could share a room," Mom said.

"Really, Jet could sleep in my room?" Darlene asked, excited at the prospect.

"No," Mom answered. "You could sleep in the doghouse with him!"

Darlene laughed and then said, "Well, I'm just going to pray about it."

A few weeks later, a young man who was enthusiastic about the Bible school plans called Dad from Brake.

"My wife and I are in the process of building an investment house about eight miles away from the Bible school property," he said. "We already own a home and the other day I said to my wife, 'I think we're building this house for the Parschauer family.' She was in total agreement and so we were wondering if you would be interested in renting our house?"

The two-story stucco home, on a hill in the village of Sommersell, overlooked a picturesque farming landscape. The front door opened to a field that led to beautiful woods. It suited our family perfectly. And God took Darlene's prayer to heart. She had a room upstairs all to herself!

That home became a haven for our family for the next years. We all loved the woods. Ken, the true naturalist in the family, spent hours there exploring with his friend Uli, who lived just down the street from us. He found and rescued an abandoned newborn bunny in the field and took such gentle care of it that "Wutzi" became a part of the family, often scampering up the steps to greet Dad studying in his office.

Dad always got up early for his quiet time, reading Scripture, meditating, and praying. Sometimes he would wake us up in the summer pre-dawn to go to the woods to listen to the birds. He knew bird calls and could mimic many of them. He must have learned some of them as a boy in Saskatchewan because he knew the sounds of meadowlarks and other prairie birds we didn't seem to find in Germany. "Keep your eyes open," he'd whisper. "You might see a deer." And we'd hold our breath, afraid to make a sound that would frighten any lovely creature away. Dad had described the thrill of gopher hunting and duck shoots in Canada, but on mornings like these, I couldn't believe he was a true hunter at heart.

Germany has lots of overcast rainy days, perfect for hiking! I loved the rain . . . the sound of it, the feel of it on your skin, and the beauty of the drops quivering on the tips of leaves, reluctant to let go.

"Darlene, it's raining; do you want to go for a walk?" I'd ask. Arms linked, we'd walk along briskly in the woods, enjoying the spongy carpet underfoot, losing track of time and, sometimes, direction. Once, we got completely lost and wandered through the woods until we finally came to the comforting sight of a solitary house in a clearing. We were bedraggled and wet, but the lady of the house invited us in and let us call home. She gave Dad directions where to find us and while we waited for him to pick us up, Darlene and I chatted with our gracious hostess and even sang her a simple hymn in German, which when translated means:

> *My God and I walk through the fields together*
> *We walk and talk as good friends should and do*
> *We clasp our hands, our voices ring with laughter*
> *My God and I walk through the meadow's hue*

The Sommersell house was not only a home for our family, but also a retreat for the Bible school students who came in groups for afternoon getaways. The winter sledding parties hosted by Dad and Mom became legendary! Dad would get truck tire tubes, which were perfect for smooth, fast, and mostly safe rides down the slopes beside our house! The students loved seeing the "director" in a less dignified role, cheering them on enthusiastically and entering into the fun. While Dad supervised the sledding, we stayed inside and helped Mom prepare the treats: "Bienenstich Kuchen" fruit tortes, apple strudel, mounds of whipped cream, and hot coffee. To help her learn the students' names, Mother would tape the picture directory of the students inside the kitchen cupboard door, and then she'd make sure to address each student by name when she served them their desserts. Years later, Dad and Mom were still getting letters from students thanking them for the memorable sledding parties at Sommersell.

Sommersell became a summer retreat over the next years while we five siblings attended college in the United States. We all scrimped and saved for airfare to Germany . . . and many friends on both sides of the ocean contributed generously so we could share those memorable family times.

Dad in his early ministry years

Mom at graduation from RN school in Toronto

Dad, his brother Willie, and his sister, Tina

Dad: young and handsome

Dad and his best friend, Ken Robins

May 10, 1944

Willie, Tina, and Dad

Newlyweds

From left to right: Donna, Dad, Johnnie, Mom, and Sharon

Winter in New Brunswick. Mother made our outfits.

New Brunswick Bible Institute Campus

Bible School in Bensheim
Our family apartment was on the second floor.

Sharon and I grew up singing and joining Dad in ministry.

Little John Jr. copying his Daddy

Dad helping me serve some Bible School guests in Bensheim

Our family in 1955
From left to right: Darlene, Dad, Sharon, Mom (holding Ken), Donna, and Johnnie

The family in 1955

Dad and Ken

From left to right: John Jr., Dad, Darlene, Sharon, Donna, Ken, Mom

Top: The picturesque town of Brake

Right: This reads, "Jesus says, 'Heaven and earth will pass away, but My words will not pass away.'"

Bibleschule Brake

The Staff at Bibleschule Brake
Far left: Ernie Klassen
Sitting in the middle: Barb McLeod
Third from left: Dad
Fourth from left: Doyle Klaassen
Far right: Heinz Weber

The student body at Bibleschule Brake
"...that in all things He might have preeminence."
Colossians 1:18 (NKJV)

The farewell celebration from Bibleschule Brake in 1978

Top: Bibleschule Brake campus

Middle Left: Photo from an album cover

Middle Right: Our family home in Sommersell

Bottom Right: Go-cart Dad and Ken built

John Mark and Sonja enjoying Christmas with Bompa

A favorite pastime

Bompa multitasking with grandbaby, Kara

Bompa with grandson, Kenny

Darlene and Dad

Ken, John, and Dad

Sharon and Dad

Donna and Dad

Kara and Bompa

Below: Bompa with grandchildren
From left to right: Andrea, John Mark, and Sonja

Left to right: Josh, Ken, Justin, Ryan, and Jonathan with Bompa

Reynell and Bompa

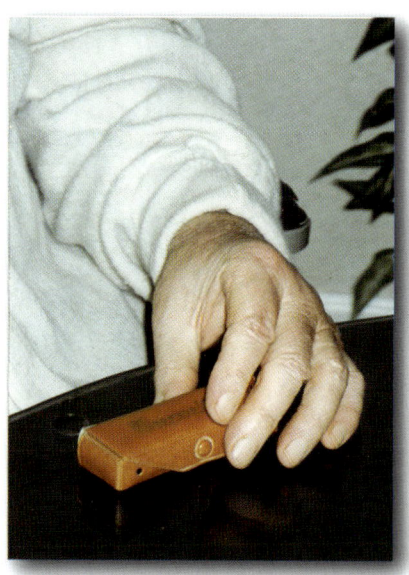

Still playing the harmonica with his one good hand

At Parkvue Health Care Center in Sandusky, Ohio

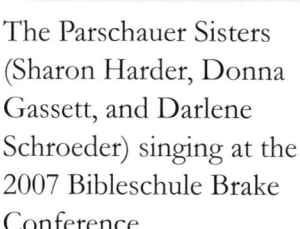

The Parschauer Sisters (Sharon Harder, Donna Gassett, and Darlene Schroeder) singing at the 2007 Bibleschule Brake Conference

Transfer of Leadership at the 2007 Conference
Left: Matthias and Imke Ruether
Right: Doyle and Lucille Klaassen

The family after Dad's funeral

Top Left: 50th Anniversary Celebration. The motto reads: *"Life in service for God."*

Top Right: Kaffetrinken (coffee and dessert) for 500 alumni at the 50th Anniversary Conference

Middle Right: Matthias and Imke Ruether with their boys during a visit in 2010

CHAPTER 10
TRANSITIONS

Whether we were all together as a family in Germany or separated by school or work responsibilities across the ocean, Dad and Mom were *with* us, either through conversations, through prayer, through phone calls, or through letters. Mother pored over our letters, underlining pertinent information and noting the names of friends that we mentioned or upcoming exams so she would remember to pray. Dad and Mom's letters were a huge source of encouragement to all of us as they followed up on the news that we had given.

As we met our future spouses and married, all five of us scheduled our weddings in either the month of August or September, when Dad was on break before the fall semester at Bible school, so he could help officiate at the ceremonies. Whenever there were significant, one of a kind events in our lives—weddings, graduations, births—Dad and Mother tried to be there. Even when they couldn't afford the trip, they trusted that if it was God's will, He would provide. Often, after they prayed about such a decision, as Dad waited to hear God's voice, Mom was already on the way, saying, "Honey, you go pray about it while I pack!"

Having grown up in an atmosphere that encouraged steps of faith, we children were open to consider mission opportunities when they arose. Sharon taught at Kent Academy in Nigeria, Africa. John and Ken did short-term medical work in Honduras. Darlene worked during the summer months with Child Evangelism Fellowship in Germany. When I was asked to teach piano at Bingham Academy in Ethiopia, I could almost hear Dad's voice encouraging me with the words of Jesus, "I tell you, open your eyes and look at the fields! They are ripe for harvest" (John 4:35 NIV).

Away from home and dependent on God alone, the faith of our parents became real to us personally. From Ethiopia, I wrote Dad and Mom that despite my fears, I was enjoying a new fresh presence of Christ that was so real that it felt almost like a "warm wall" around me. They were so encouraged by the news because my words echoed exactly what they had been praying for me. Concerned for my protection in the politically volatile atmosphere of Ethiopia at that time, they had been praying this verse: "'For I,' says the LORD, 'will be a wall of fire all around her, and I will be the glory in her midst'" (Zechariah 2:5 NKJV). The words "warm wall" in my letter confirmed for them that God was indeed answering their prayers.

Dad and Mother had no specific plans about where they would retire, but they had decided to hand over the leadership of the Bible school when Dad turned 65. Doyle Klaassen, a young man from Saskatchewan, was to become the new director. Like Dad, Doyle was a graduate of Pambrun Bible Institute and a godly, capable, and respected teacher and leader. Over the years, Dad and Mother had forged a deep bond with Doyle and his lovely wife, Lucille, and their four children. And Dad was convinced that Doyle was the man with the heart, skill, and humility to continue and expand the work of the Bible school in Germany. Doyle was reluctant at first, but with Dad's encouragement and much prayer, he accepted the directorship, which Dad gladly and gratefully relinquished.

And so, in 1978, hundreds of students and alumni who considered Dad their spiritual father honored him and Mother at a moving farewell celebration in Brake. The service featured a procession of over 50 flags representing the countries in which graduates are serving as missionaries. And so, as a history of Bibelschule Brake titled *Gott ist Treu (God is Faithful)* stated, "By God's grace, a simple Canadian prairie farmer became one of the most renowned missionaries and Bible teachers in Germany."

Just as Dad and Mom had lived by faith for years as missionaries, they trusted God for their next steps. With no home in the United States and no significant retirement fund, we siblings wondered how God would provide. But soon after his retirement, Dad accepted an offer to become part-time missions representative for Word of Life International in Schroon Lake, New York. (Dad had encouraged "Wort des Lebens" in Germany from the very beginning, when the Word of Life Quartet began their ministry there.)

Dad and Mom were still looking and praying for accommodations in Schroon Lake when a letter came from a businessman in Germany who was writing, he said, on behalf of a group of German Christians expressing appreciation for Dad's and Mom's 25 years of service to their country. Enclosed with the letter was enough money for a large down payment on a lovely house, the first home Dad and Mother ever owned.

The home became a magnet for family vacations over the next few years. Christmas celebrations at "Nana and Bompa's" were highlights for their 10 grandchildren. Tea parties, snow tubing at the local golf course, games of Rook, hikes up Mount Severance—what fun to have Dad and Mom on this side of the Atlantic Ocean!

They still made mission trips to encourage Bible school alumni. One trip took them to Lisbon, Portugal in May 1981. Dad and Mother's 37th anniversary happened to fall during that time, and Dad made sure he didn't miss the chance to celebrate the occasion in spite of the busy ministry schedule. The anniversary coincided with Mother's Day that year, so Dad wrote Mother this poem:

How good the Lord has been to me
To place you at my side
Just thirty-seven years ago
You became my loving bride
These many years we've traveled
Over hill and dale, over plain and sea
We've witnessed God's good hand
In many a country
On this glad day in Portugal
I love you even more
Than on the day the Lord united us
On that Canadian shore
This also being Mother's Day
I do want you to know
That not only I but all our children
Love and adore you so
We all wish you God's special grace
Abiding peace and rest
And would not wait until "someday"
To call our treasure "blessed."

Dad and Mother were fully engaged in the lives of their children and grandchildren. Mother was famous for her waffle breakfasts, coconut tarts, and her toast-and-tea parties. Her grandchildren knew that Nana would always be delighted whenever they surprised her at the door. For their granddaughters, they made doll houses complete with carpeted rooms. For the boys, Bompa made slingshots and other toys in his basement workshop. One day I overheard our daughter, Sonja, in tears on the phone telling Mom her pet hamster, Smoky, had just died. An hour later, Bompa and Nana were at our front door holding a perfectly crafted miniature coffin covered and lined with purple corduroy and decorated with petunias. They took a little girl's loss seriously and even participated in a formal backyard burial service for Smokey. In practical ways, the life of Jesus flowed graciously through "Nana and Bompa."

CHAPTER 11
FOR THIS I HAVE JESUS

The grace continued to flow when Mom was stricken with aggressive pancreatic cancer in 1991. The reality that Mother would not be with us for much longer was absolutely devastating for the whole family. She faded away quickly before our eyes, but her courage and faith seemed to get even stronger. On particularly difficult and painful days, she would often tell us, "For this I have Jesus."

It was a privilege to care for her in her home. When she could eat nothing but ice chips, we served them to her in tiny Royal Doulton china cups. Presentation was always important to Mom. And she was quick to express her appreciation: "Just lovely, dear; so refreshing." She never lost her sense of humor, either. One morning I threw on an old bathrobe of Mom's and went to her bedroom to greet her.

"A new robe?" she quipped.

"No," I answered, "This robe has clothed beautiful women down through the ages."

"Well then, why are *you* wearing it!?"

But there was crushing sadness too. One night, I woke in Dad and Mom's guest bedroom. It was 4 a.m. and I was feeling the unbearable weight and grief of losing Mom. I stifled my sobs so I wouldn't be heard. I couldn't get back to sleep, so I tiptoed downstairs and stood in front of the window watching the snow fall lightly outside in the predawn. I turned around to see Dad coming down the hallway. Instantly, he read my face and my heart. We hugged in wordless understanding. After a while Dad said, "Now, why don't you go back to sleep." Suddenly I was 5 again, and my Daddy was taking care of me. So, almost instinctively, I responded. I walked upstairs, got into bed, and fell asleep.

A few days before Easter, all 10 grandchildren filed into Nana's room to say goodbye. She had begun sewing Easter bunnies for each of them but was too weak to finish. Sharon took over the job and gave Mom the joy of giving each one of the children one last gift. As the children left Nana's bedroom, Darlene noticed Mom was trying to say something and bent down to catch the words.

"What was that, Mom?"

In a faint voice, Mother repeated the words: "So many things to celebrate." At the funeral home on April 23, 1992, my brother, Ken, overheard his 8-year-old son, Josh, singing. Ken asked him to sing the words again for me—a spontaneously composed expression of his heart. I quickly wrote down the words on the back of an envelope:

Why did you have to go
Why did you have to go so soon?
Why couldn't you stay and play
Why did you have to take that heavenly hot air balloon?
For all I know you could be dancin'; you could be prancin'
You could be doing somersaults
For all I know you could be singin'
You could be eating chocolate malts
But, Nana, why did you have to go . . .

Doyle Klaassen traveled from Germany to speak at the funeral. "Uncle" Mark Bredin and "Auntie" Ruth Robins came all the way from New Brunswick Bible Institute to pay tribute to Mother and to support Dad. My husband, Bill, wrote a poem that he read at the service:

Her Love and Her Laughter

God gave us a beautiful lady
God gave us a wonderful friend
Her life here on earth is now over
But her love and her laughter won't end

What memories we have of her kindness
Her generous and unselfish way
Her sweet gentle voice may be gone now
But her love and her laughter will stay

She cared for our children with wisdom
We never once heard her complain
They'll miss Nana reading them stories
But her love and her laughter remain

Each meal she made was a banquet
Even her tea and her toast
We'll cherish her tarts and her waffles
But her love and her laughter the most

She lived like the lady in Proverbs
Whose hands were kept busy with cheer
Her sewing machine is now silent
But her love and her laughter we hear

Much more could be said about Nana
How she played with the kids in the snow
Like flowers some memories may fade
But her love and her laughter will grow

We're grateful for all she has taught us
Her life was a fruitful tree
Her faith, hope, and courage a treasure
But her love and her laughter the key

She's loving and laughing in glory
Now that she's home with the King
We can't take possessions to heaven
But her love and her laughter we'll bring

A family friend, Shirley Cooman, read short tributes from each of the 10 grandchildren. Six-year-old Kara's was concise. Only eight poignant words: "I wish you didn't die until next Easter."

THROUGH THE VALLEY

Dad showed amazing courage in his grief. He missed Mother terribly, but instead of retreating into self-pity, he reached out toward his grandchildren and took over some of Nana's traditions—taking them individually out for breakfast; attending their concerts, baseball games, and soccer games; and even inviting them to his apartment for sleepovers!

His thoughtfulness was often expressed through letters and poetry. When he was almost 80, he wrote "A Tribute to our Son Ken":

From Bensheim in West Germany in 1955
I drove our car to Darmstadt without a front-wheel drive

To reach our goal—the hospital—driving through slush and snow and cold
In order to deliver what was more precious far than gold

My own Maureen, then great with child, weary, tired, and worn
Anxiously awaiting our fifth child to be born

Now in a foreign country her heart was strangely stirred
She had studied French in high school; German she had never heard

Anxiety was soon forgotten when the doctor said with joy
I'm happy to announce to you: you have a baby boy

One person was especially glad almost more than Mother
It was John who earnestly had prayed that he might have a brother

He wanted him to grow up fast with pants made out of leather
In weather, though oft overcast, they then could play together

We decided to call our baby Ken in memory of Ken Robins
Who to me so often had been a help in solving problems

When not quite two years old one day to demonstrate his skill
Ken walked back and forth on second floor outside on window sill!

While gasping neighbors passing by were shocked at what they saw
His mother's heart, near petrified, could only stare in awe

For This I Have Jesus

But faithful Barbara MacLeod got up there just in time
To snatch him near the baby crib from where he'd made his climb

While speeding with his tricycle not really all his fault
He ran into a drainage trap and came to a sudden halt

Less two front teeth we picked him up: cause for concern and prayer
He looked for many days that followed like a swollen little bear

When Wilhelm left for mission work and determined there to stay
He left his motor bike with us to sell or give away

There seemed to be no interest in a motorbike that old
When no one took it as a gift, it was, of course, not sold

When coming home from school one day, we watched a soap-box race
An idea flashed through our minds, a thought not hard to trace

The dump near by—not far away—supplied us all we needed
It wasn't too long after that we had indeed succeeded

The frame, some six feet in length, the wheelbase four feet wide
Old scooter wheels in front, rears from the bike, gave Kenneth quite a ride

To watch his trial run one day had gathered quite a crowd
Upon his return, his face revealed that he was rather proud

As ophthalmologist today he's usually very busy
Time to relax is racing cars . . . to watch then makes one dizzy

In a qualifying race one day it was really quite a feat
With windshield smashed and injured nose, wild turkeys on his seat

Reminiscing now of days gone by how could we ever forget
Our early strolls together and your baby rabbit pet

When long before the break of day just you and I would stroll
To nearby woods, watch ducks and deer, or hear the cuckoo call

Some say that the cuckoo bird is often hard to see
We watched them, some on nearby shrubs and at times on towering tree.

Of the many varied memories one has forever stuck
When you on that frosty morning sneaked up on a full-grown buck

When head and horns would disappear to get a bit more to eat
As quietly as possible you'd sneak a few more feet

Until you were just yards away it gave me quite a scare
When with a funny noise the deer jumped high into the air

He stomped his foot on frozen ground re-echoing far and near
Then with long jumps he disappeared to join the other deer

Remember on that Easter morn, holidays had just begun
A service with our family at the rising of the sun

A lack of fear was manifest in a variety of ways
A Tarzan jump to the unknown caused you to limp for days

Vacations spent in Italy on the Adriatic Sea
In six feet of nice warm water the bottom you could see

Building castles on the beach with moats and towers all of sand
Or catching trout from babbling brooks just with your own bare hand

How precious are those memories of helping Mother bake
Those delicious chocolate cookies or her famous Whacky Cake

Her specialty was waffles in shape of Valentine hearts
Enjoyed by all who ate them like her tasty coconut tarts

How comforting it was to know that God does love us still
Even when we were all informed that Mother was so ill

Your support to me meant more than I can ever tell
When health conditions clearly showed her case was terminal

When Mother expressed her own desire to fight cancer another way
You accompanied her to Germany almost the following day

When soon it became evident nothing further could be done
We all took care of her right here until God took her home

The bunny rabbits she had made with tiny stitches fine
Were presented to each grandchild as they filed by in line

Each gave a kiss to Nana with a teardrop in each eye
They really meant "aufwiederseh'n" by saying their goodbye

The next day was Easter Monday before the rising of the sun
Her earthly race had ended; her Master said "Well done."

To you and my whole family, whatever may be your ranks
I want to express to God and you my deepest, heartfelt thanks.

A few months after Mother's funeral, my sister, Sharon, accompanied Dad on a memorable trip to New Brunswick to give him the opportunity to visit the many friends who had supported us through the years. That trip was to become the last farewell.

CHAPTER 12
DAD'S LAST BATTLE

Dad faced his toughest physical challenge on November 7, a year and a half after Mom died—a severe stroke which impaired his speech and paralyzed his right side. Literally overnight, he went from total independence to utter dependence. After weeks of occupational, physical, and speech therapy, he still required full-time care and was transferred to a care facility.

Not being able to talk frustrated Dad more than anything. For someone whose whole life had been speaking, singing, and preaching, the sudden limitation was devastating. Sitting on his bedside one day, sensing his frustration and feeling helpless myself, I asked, "Daddy, do you think you can hum?" He said "I don't know" with shrugged shoulders and questioning eyes and then tried to hum. After the first few tentative notes, I recognized the tune and joined him, singing the words while he hummed. "Take the name of Jesus with you, child of sorrow and of woe . . . Precious Name, O how sweet, hope of earth and joy of heaven." We finished our duet, both burst into tears and I kissed, kissed his cheek. I knew I had just participated in a sacred commissioning service, a call to carry on the legacy of taking the name of Jesus into all the world.

With more speech therapy, Dad improved a little. He even began joking with the therapist. She'd point to pictures or words, for instance "money" and he'd say, "Don't have any!" One day she commented on a minor cut on his head, and he quipped, "You should see the other guy!"

But eventually, Dad's speech and physical abilities declined. He was confined to a wheelchair and had no use of his right arm. I remember him saying in sermons that he'd love to be active and preaching until God took him home. But God had a different design for Dad's last days. He had lost so much by then: the woman who had supported and delighted him for almost 48 years, his material possessions, his health, his independence, his mobility, and his speech. But even in his diminished physical condition and in spite of occasional discouragement, for another seven years Dad maintained a powerful life of ministry and influence.

The grace that characterized his life still flowed from him to others. He never lost his ability to speak the words "Thank you." And he never lost his courteous charm. It was customary for him to gallantly tip his hat to the women in the lobby as we wheeled him toward the doors for a walk outside.

Before his stroke, Dad had been known for delighting family members and friends with birthday phone calls in which he would play "Happy Birthday" on his harmonica. Once, during my sister Darlene's almost-daily visits, she noticed the unused harmonica in a drawer, picked it up and asked, "Can you try playing this, Daddy?" At first he shook his head no, but then he took it with his good hand. Looking uncertain, his blue eyes fixed on Darlene's face, he tried a few tentative notes. With her encouragement and his own dear persistence, the song reemerged. And the birthday calls continued to surprise and bless!

Dad's lifelong friends supported him through letters and prayer. He had always written regularly to them, so on his behalf I wrote a newsletter to them:

January 27, 1997:

Dear friends of Dad Parschauer,

Many of you have been wondering about and praying for Dad. We have been touched by the way you have expressed your care through letters and cards. It's been over three years now since Dad's stroke left him paralyzed and very limited in speech, but let me assure you that this soldier is still fighting the good fight! His mind is quite alert and his spirit alive.

Recently, I read him the first two chapters of Daniel from his own well-worn Bible. One carefully underlined passage in chapter 2 brought from him a burst of emotion:

"Praise be to the name of God for ever and ever; wisdom and power are his. He changes times and seasons; he sets up kings and deposes them. He gives wisdom to the wise and knowledge to the discerning. He

reveals deep and hidden things; He knows what lies in darkness and light dwells with him. I thank and praise you, O God of my fathers."

Hidden things, darkness . . . yes. And they are distressing, like the concussion from his motorized scooter accident, the constant dependence on aides for every move involving bed, wheelchair and toilet, the frustration of not being able to say what you want to. But also light! What a blessing Dad continues to be! At church, when "the patriarch" is wheeled in, people are drawn to him like to a magnet . . . especially children who greet him with "Hi, Bompa," and reach for his extended "good" hand.

Because of Dad, we enjoy a whole network of relationships with aides, nurses, doctors, therapists, and residents, many of whom have come to the Chapel and to the Christmas functions the Chapel has sponsored. My piano students gave their Christmas recital at Dad's health care center and then helped decorate his Christmas tree.

Recently, a resident across the hallway passed away and the family members requested that our family lead the memorial service. Over one hundred people filled the care center's chapel as Darlene, Sonja (our daughter), and I sang; Bill gave the message; and John Jr. and his wife, Beverly, participated in prayer and piano music. Dad offered the touch of Jesus through his tears.

Dad has almost daily interaction with family members and friends. One of Dad's chief pleasures seems to be food! His waistline proves it. So restaurant outings are fun. He eats meticulously with his left hand. He is a part of almost every family celebration. At Thanksgiving, Dad even played Rook with a little help from Darlene! Four of his five children live near him: John and Ken as respected ophthalmologists with Parschauer Eye Center; Darlene as pastor's wife to Bill Schroeder giving leadership to The Chapel in Sandusky, which averages over four hundred in attendance; and Bill and I, who divide our time between Crescendo Ministries and The Chapel. Sharon and her husband, David Harder, a businessman in Schroon Lake, New York, come to visit whenever possible. Four of the 10 grandchildren are now in college. Five of them attended Urbana Missions conference with almost 20,000 other students, which thrilled Dad's missionary heart!

There have been some highlight visits from friends in Germany: Doyle Klaassen, who followed Dad as president of the Brake Bible School; Maria Ehrhard, Dad's secretary for 20 years; the Timblins, from Brake; the German Word of Life Quartet; "Auntie" Barb MacLeod; graduates from the Bible schools in both Germany and Canada . . . .

I'm going to go and see Dad now. I'll probably find him in the foyer sitting close to the warm fireplace. As I walk through the automatic doors, I'll give our family whistle and he'll look up with a pleased smile. We'll read together or play a game or recite Scripture verses (with him kicking in the words I set up) and then we may pay one of his friends in another room a visit. When I leave, he'll accompany me back to the foyer, kiss my hand, and say, "thank you," one of the few phrases he can still enunciate clearly. I'll hug him. Then, according to ritual, he'll stay at the picture window and wave with his white handkerchief as I slowly drive under the portico returning his wave.

I hope that through this update you are hearing Dad's "thank you" for your prayers and fellowship. One day soon, his wheelchair will be for sale. His saxophone will join the trumpet sound and we'll all spend eternity together . . . .

Praising the Name of Jesus,

Donna

During the final days of Dad's life, our family kept constant vigil, tried to make him as comfortable as possible, read to him, and sang as a family around his bedside. Nurses, aides, and residents kept coming into his room to say goodbye. One aide kept repeating, "John changed my life, John changed my life." Abused by her own father, she'd found in Dad a gentle father figure. She told us that sometimes she would just stand in Dad's room to soak in the peace that filled its atmosphere. So many others wrote letters of thanks to Dad expressing how he had touched their lives. One letter was particularly poignant, written by a woman in ministry:

Dear Mr. Parschauer,

…Memories of my time with you and your family are among the most dear to me. I treasure each recollection I have with you and Maureen. Your gracious way of opening up your home…the way you made everyone feel like royalty, even if you served a simple cup of tea…your listening skills, the genuine caring…well, words can't convey the impact you have had. Over the years, I have been asked who my mentors are. (Often it's been phrased, "Who would you like to be when you grow up?") My answer is always: "John and Maureen Parschauer." When days have been rough and my time in the valley long and wearisome, I could have wandered toward the pit of despair and wondered where God was. But always, your faces would appear in my memory. I could not dispute the loving heart of God, for I had seen Him alive in your eyes, hands, and hearts. Without knowing it, you passed on your legacy to me. Because of both of you, I am aware of the power of Christ-filled encouragement. I am quick to extend God's heart to others. I know it will be life-changing because I have been on the receiving end of your heart.

Also, I want you to know that your godly walk lives on in more ways than you can imagine. Years ago, while having tea with Donna, she shared a story with me. She told me of a time when she was five. She sat with Sharon in the front row of a church in Germany while you preached. Midway through your sermon, you looked down and noticed she was tired. Instead of continuing with your message, you excused yourself from the platform, went down to where she was sitting, and helped her make a place to lie down. You then covered her up with your suitcoat and went back and continued speaking. I don't know what your text was that evening, but I'm confident of the message the people took home with them that night. I have been sharing that story for years since then. It describes so beautifully the nature of our heavenly Father. It allows people to see how their Father cherishes them, how He notices when they're too fragile to walk on their own. It introduces them to a God who is not consumed with the "big, important" things so much that He fails to be centered on each of His children….

> *How can I begin to tell you how powerfully God has used your example in my life. Your walk as a father has allowed others to fall in love with their heavenly Father for the first time. For many years, I was unable to share this story without choking up and finding myself unable to continue. I guess each of us has our scars…It's because of this that your life has touched me so…*

Dad always rose early in the morning, along with the birds, to meet with his Lord. So it was fitting that on Thursday, June 1, 2000, as the birds began their dawn chorus, Dad should meet with His Lord, this time face to face. I am quite sure a little Irish woman was waiting to meet him, with coffee already poured.

The funeral was a beautiful celebration of God's faithfulness to a man who had finished the race with rare integrity and grace. Doyle Klaassen again travelled from Germany with his wife, Lucille. They managed to arrive in time to be at Dad's bedside before his death. At the funeral, Doyle eloquently honored Dad, summarizing his ministry and picturing him perfectly:

> *From our hearts, Lucille and I want to extend to you, the Parschauer family, our sympathy as you mourn the loss of your father and grandfather. At the same time, we all happily realize that he is now in heaven with Jesus, who forgave his sins and gave him eternal life. He's reunited with all who, like him, trusted Jesus and have died, especially with your Mother, with Nana. Now he's using that right hand again, walking, whistling, and speaking. This is a day to celebrate, to shout like we did at the division finals when the Sandusky boys ran so well and Bompa's grandson, Ryan, long-jumped to victory. It's a day to throw our hats in the air, to wave, and be happy.*
>
> *I stand before you today representing literally thousands of people in Germany who knew and respected and loved "Herr Parschauer." Please allow me to say just one sentence to his five children in the language of their childhood days: Gnade sei mit euch und Friede von Gott unsrem Vater und von dem Herrn Jesus Christus. (Grace be with you and peace from God our Father and from the Lord Jesus Christ.)*
>
> *For almost a quarter of a century, Germany was home to the Parschauer family as they responded to God's call for service there. Soon after World War II, in 1949, many Christian leaders desiring to take the gospel to the ends of the earth met in Switzerland for a Congress on World Evangelism. Among*

Dad's Last Battle

them most notably, the young Youth for Christ evangelist Billy Graham and the man whom we remember especially today. There and then, and during another summer stint to the continent, a vision to start a Bible School in war-torn Germany was born. In 1954, the Parschauer Family left by boat for Europe. Under the auspices of Greater Europe Mission, John started a Bible Institute, which continues to operate with blessing to this day. Then, in 1959, he and Maureen, fellow-Canadians Ernie and Erma Klassen, and Heinz Weber, later joined by Irmgard, started what was to become the Bibelschule Brake, which he led so ably for 19 years. Little did he realize that this school would become the largest of its kind not only in Germany but in all of Europe.

John Parschauer had a passion for world missions. He wanted everyone to know that God's Son, Jesus, had died and risen from the grave to bring salvation to all who believe in Him. Today, graduates of Brake are carrying that glorious message of life and hope as missionaries to 65 countries around the globe. John was also key initiator of the intermissions conference, which drew hundreds of missionaries together for one week every year to enjoy fellowship and the preaching of the Word. Even more significantly, I believe, he helped organize a conference for evangelical theological schools which today serves the interests of some 30 institutions of learning.

As the one who followed in John's footsteps as the leader of the Bibelschule Brake, I know firsthand of the high regard in which many other Christian leaders hold him and how his former students revere him.

I share all this today for many of you who worship here at the Chapel in these last seven years have known him only as a saintly, white-haired invalid in a wheelchair, hardly able to speak, but endowed with an almost inexplicable magnetism that attracted young and old alike and wordlessly pointed them to Christ the Savior.

Let me share a few random favorite memories of John Parschauer, whom I have known for some 45 years and under whose leadership I grew as a Christian and a minister.

John loved to play a game of Rook. I can see him now whistling silently as he takes the kitty, bluffs with a hand that has almost nothing in it and then makes his bid repeatedly to become the chuckling winner of the evening.

I see him skating on the frozen winter pond in Sommersell, handling that hockey stick with dexterity reminiscent of the skill of earlier days.

And again: Lucille and I leave almost 80-year-old John, now widowed, with our youngest two teenage children, asking him to share his testimony with them in evening devotions while we go off to an appointment. The next morning Denise reports, "Mr. Parschauer talked for almost an hour, but, Dad, it wasn't the least bit boring."

In my next memory I'm a single missionary, back in the 60s. A phone call from home informs me that my father has been taken to the hospital. Suddenly, I hear that unmistakable knock at my door and the Parschauers join in my pain. Maureen talks confidently with the reassuring medical knowledge of her profession and then we hold hands while John shoulders my burden and brings it to the Lord in prayer.

Holding hands and praying. We were constantly doing that. We'd have spent another evening at the Parschauer home in Sommersell. Come leaving time and with our coats on, we'd stand in a circle at the door and John would pray. He was never far away from the Lord with whom he walked humbly and uprightly, yes, and naturally, for he trusted the Savior implicitly.

Three things marked John Parschauer, I think, as I look back on his life from my perspective now. First of all, his deep faith in Christ. For people who might think that a man with his character traits would automatically make heaven, I must protest on his behalf. John knew how much he stood in need of God's grace. We have knelt together in our living room—just he and I—in deep awareness of our need to ask again for the gracious assurance that the blood of Jesus Christ covers all our sins.

Then, John had a deep interest in and concern for other people. Nobody was just a number to him. He treated everyone with dignity and respect. Recently, I met a man who reached back over 30 years and brought up whole conversations revealing a busy director who had taken the time to explain the gospel in such a clear way that he still knows it today.

For people who knew John intimately, his humility stood out boldly. Among the hundreds of missionaries whom I have known in Europe in three and a half decades, few have served as effectively as John Parschauer did when judged from our human vantage point. For many, he became a living legend. Standing in our garage door one day as we looked back over his leadership years which I knew to be so effective, John offered this explanation: "I just kinda bluffed my way through." He was wrong on that, for the Bible says, "God resists the proud but gives grace to the humble." God is the explanation for the life we honor today.

Finally, I want you to think of two verses from the Bible. The first one could have been written by John Parschauer himself: "Then King David went in and sat before the Lord and he said, Who am I, O sovereign Lord, and what is my family, that you have brought me this far?" (II Samuel 7:18; NIV)

And the second would be my wish for all of us. "Remember your leaders, who spoke the Word of God to you. Consider the outcome of their way of life and imitate their faith. Jesus Christ is the same yesterday, and today and forever." (Hebrews 13:7–8; NIV)

There were other touching tributes, one given by Danny Robins (son of Dad's lifelong friend, Ken Robins), who with his wife, Lorna, represented the New Brunswick Bible Institute family. Rev. Jim Jeffery, a pastor from Grand Rapids, Michigan and now president of Baptist Bible Seminary, spoke on behalf of the young men and women in ministry who had been encouraged by Dad. Jim said that Dad had told him years before, "Always preach to broken hearts and you'll never lack an audience."

Sharon, Darlene, and I sang and, as spokesperson for the family, I shared some of our favorite things about Dad: his whistle, his love of nature, the handmade dollhouses, go-carts, pet-caskets, window-boxes, car trips interrupted by games of hide and seek, teaching us to sing and love music, his dry wit and arsenal of puns and jokes that we all knew by heart, his birthday greetings played over the phone on saxophone and after the stroke with his one good hand, on harmonica…the many ways he found to show us he loved us.

Via video, Dad played at his own service! A recording of his saxophone music accompanied a video commemorating his life. Pastor Bill Schroeder even included in his message a short recorded excerpt of Dad preaching and offering the gospel. At the graveside, after the final prayer, a flock of Canadian geese flew in formation low over the tent as if on cue—a perfect aerial salute.

In many of Dad's letters over the years he would add an acronym after his signature: LFW: "Let's finish well." There's no doubt. He did.

And the legacy goes on . . . Thank you, Bompa.

"When the sun goes below the horizon he is not set; the heavens glow for a full hour after his departure. And when a great and good man sets, the sky of this world is luminous long after he is out of sight. Such a man cannot die out of this world. When he goes he leaves behind him much of himself. Being dead, he speaks." Henry Ward Beecher

The Sun Rises and It Sets

By Sonja Gassett

In memory of Bompa,
builder of Bible schools, dollhouses, and my heritage of faith

The sun rises and it sets
When it rises the whole world is a canvas waiting to be painted
Bright colors fill the air

Every life is a sunrise, is a sunset

The sun rises and it sets
When it sets the whole world seems drained of its color
Only blues and grays remain

Every life is a sunrise, is a sunset

And God calls for the righteous
And God carries them home

The sun rises and it sets
When it rises, all heaven, all heaven, all heaven
Is a canvas painted with glory
Never-fading glory

(Recorded on "Broken but Beautiful")

Other Words and Music Inspired by John and Maureen Parschauer

If I Were Big and You Were Little

By Andrea Schroeder…in memory of Bompa

I remember the day 20 years ago when I walked down those basement stairs…the ones I loved to sit on and look through all your books that lined the wall. The books were so worn and well used; they felt so important and distinguished.

I walked down those stairs to your office toting my own worn and important book, "Rainy Day Circus." Even though I knew the book by heart, I still loved the way it sounded with your voice reading the lines. On this day, though, I think you had a lot of other things to do and didn't have enough time to read a book to me, until I said, "Bompa, if I was big and you were little, I would read to you."

Today, a lot of things have changed, but that line still rings in my head: Bompa, if I was big and you were little…

If I was big and you were little…
> I would build you a dollhouse, or a wooden truck, or a rubber band gun
> I would snap my fingers and fascinate you or whistle a tune to brighten your day
> I would take you out to lunch and tell you about Jesus using the most amazing little paper tricks or other unique objects

If I was big and you were a teen…
> I would be the one you could always count on for a Werther's candy or a snack (you wouldn't mind if it was a little stale, would you?)
> I would write you poems for your birthday
> I would instill in you a love for the Bible, a passion to know it by heart
> I would show you how to grieve with dignity
>   and the peace that only Jesus can bring

If I was big and you were a young adult…
> I would teach you that God chooses to use you in every circumstance and that there is not a place or condition that can inhibit your ministry
> I would light up your day with a smile and "thank you," even if that was all I could do
> I would have picnics with you by the water, enjoying the boats, the geese, and the peace of being outside

I would show you what it was like to live a life with no regrets
I would leave you with an amazing legacy:
    a love for the Lord,
    a passion for telling the world about a God,
    a mother who through her joy in serving is the picture
    of true love

Bompa, if I was big and you were little, I hope I would be the hero to you that you have been to me.

The Father's Gift
Words by Donna Gassett
Recorded by the Parschauer Sisters on "Candlelight Christmas"
...in loving memory of Dad Parschauer

As candles flickered on the tree Daddy handed down to me
One tiny gift, a box without a bow
I looked up with grand surprise at the tears in his eyes
For the box held a locket: a treasure of gold

How can I thank him at Christmas time
For Love come down from his hand
I will take that precious gold
And evermore I will hold it close to my heart
I know he'll understand

The heavenly Father gives today gifts that take our breath away
High mountain peaks and rivers running cold
But can you see the Father's eyes as heaven made the sacrifice
One tiny Baby, more precious than gold

How can I thank Him at Christmas time
For Love come down from His hand
I will take that precious Gold
And evermore I will hold it close to my heart
I know He'll understand

So Much to Celebrate
Words and Music by Donna and Sonja Gassett
Recorded on "Broken but Beautiful"

Came home from school with a smile on my face;
I had aced the test
Mama lit a candle, put the teapot on; and then she said
"Let's have a party like the time we did
When you won the race…like you hoped you would
There's so much to celebrate, celebrate."

Came home from school with a tear in my eye;
I had flunked the test
Mama lit a candle, put the teapot on; and then she said:
"Let's have a party like the time we did
When you lost the race…but you ran to win
There's so much to celebrate, celebrate."

Mama has run her final race; we were gathered around her bed
We light a candle, kiss her goodbye; then Mama says:
"We'll have a party in my new home
Where we'll sing together around the throne;
There's so much to celebrate, celebrate."
Forever we will celebrate, celebrate.

Tiny Stitches
By Donna Gassett
…remembering Mom, Maureen Parschauer

Heading out the door to catch the bus in time for school
He suddenly remembered something he forgot to do
"Mom," he called in panic, "do you think that you could sew
This emblem on my jacket before I have to go?"

That night as she was tucking all the children into bed
He pointed to the emblem on the jacket and then said,
"Mom, you used such big stitches and I guess it's fine
But didn't you say that tiny ones mean more than work and time."

Tiny, tiny stitches
Spell love with needle and with thread
Tiny, tiny stitches
More eloquent than any words she said

Later on she tiptoed softly back in to the room
And picked up that old jacket from the floor where it was strewn
Then taking off the emblem she sewed it on again
Using tiny stitches where those big ones had been

TRIBUTE TO MY FATHER
by Dr. John Parschauer

Words often fail to express the deep love, respect, and gratitude I have for my dear Dad, but I will summarize some of my feelings as follows:

F - Faithful, Forgiving, Friend, Follower of Christ
A - Abiding (John 15 - "abide in me"), Accountable, Adored Mom
T - Trustworthy, True, Tolerant, Terrific Dad
H - Humble, Helpful, Honest, Honorable
E - Easy to talk to, to love and a steady Example
R - Respectful, Respected, Reverent, Revered, Reverend

**THANKS DAD - MY MENTOR, MY HERO, MY FATHER
I DEEPLY LOVE AND RESPECT YOU!
YOUR SON, JOHN**

TRIBUTE TO BOMPA
by John Mark Parschauer Jr.

Let's Finish Well

A vision to teach from the Word brings a year to learn.
A man will grow to lead.
Spirit, song, we follow You.
Let's finish well.

Love will lead my heart to yours.
My life, to you and ours.
As I go, so shall I cherish you.
Let's finish well.

With these young hearts in our care,
Learn to love.
Learn to be.
Live to serve through Him.

As I walk.
As I bring my soul to act justly.
And to love mercy.
And to walk humbly with my God.
Let's finish well.

Why Did You Have to Go
Josh Parschauer (age 8) for Nana

Why did you have to go?
Why did you have to go so soon?
Why couldn't you stay and play
Why did you have to take that heavenly hot air balloon?
For all I know you could be dancin'; you could be prancin'
You could be doing somersaults
For all I know you could be singin'
You could be eating chocolate malts
But, Nana, why did you have to go so soon
Why couldn't you stay and play
Why did you have to take that heavenly hot air balloon?

EPILOGUE

2012

John Parschauer's legacy of faith lives on. "Bibelschule Brake," the Bible school in Germany that he helped to found, is the largest evangelical Bible college in Germany. In 2007, Doyle Klaassen handed the position of director over to Matthias Ruether, a well-qualified young German, under whose leadership the school is continuing to thrive. The theme verse for the college is still 2 Timothy 2:2: ". . . now teach these truths to other trustworthy people who will be able to pass them on to others" (NLT). More than two thousand young people have graduated from the school and are serving in ministries worldwide. What a privilege it was for us as a family to attend the 50th anniversary celebration of the Bible school in 2009. We (The Parschauer Sisters) were invited to sing and John Jr. to give words of greeting. Dad's life was remembered and honored in many ways. One of the students played a tribute saxophone solo, giving an authentic version of one of Dad's hymn arrangements. An emotional moment came with the surprise video recording of Dad giving a report about the miraculous beginnings of the school. One afternoon during the conference, five hundred alumni gathered for "Kaffeetrinken" (coffee and desserts) and testimonies of God's faithfulness. Dad would have loved it!

After 50 years, The New Brunswick Bible Institute (NBBI) in Canada is as committed as ever in 2011 to its mission: to make godly disciples and devoted servant leaders for Jesus Christ . . . men and women of character, wisdom, and discernment who will impact the world with the Gospel of God. A recent visiting speaker, Dr. Ray Pritchard, described NBBI as "an amazing place, an undiscovered jewel among the Bible institutes in North America. From this rural hillside in New Brunswick, they are training the next generation of Christian leaders."

Danny Robins, the son of Dad's best friend, Ken, serves as business manager there and helps keep the Parschauer/Robins connection strong with personal letters written with his father's inherited eloquence and always signed "LFW" (Let's finish well).

Dad's legacy lives on in the lives of his children and grandchildren. Sharon teaches grade school and, besides her work in the church, uses her extraordinary decorating and event planning skills in community outreaches. She and her husband, David Harder, a businessman, have two children (Reynell Smith and Jonathan), both medical doctors.

Donna and Bill Gassett, involved in songwriting, singing, and speaking under Crescendo Ministries, live in Huron, Ohio. Donna is director of music at The Chapel in Sandusky. Bill and Donna's daughter (Sonja Leavitt) is a singer-songwriter and a worship leader. She also teaches at Ohio State University (OSU) in Columbus.

John Jr. is an ophthalmologist (Parschauer Eye Center) in Sandusky, Ohio, where he and his wife, Beverly, raised their three sons: John Mark, a musician; Justin, a doctor; and Ryan, a hospice chaplain. Both John and Beverly serve actively in The Chapel and in the community and have been involved in medical mission trips.

Darlene, married to Bill Schroeder, who founded and pastors The Chapel in Sandusky, helps nurture the congregation, which has grown to two thousand over the past 25 years. She shares vitally in the vision for ministry and serves the heart of the church with her sensitivity to people. She is gifted in creating an environment of warmth and hospitality and involved in worship, production, staging, and design. She and Bill have two children: Andrea Preston, a pediatrician; and Ken, studying criminal justice.

Ken and his wife, Lucy, also live in Sandusky, Ohio. Ken is an ophthalmologist at Parschauer Eye Center and specializes in cataract surgery. He has worked with the Christian Medical Society performing many surgeries in third world countries. He has two children: Josh, a copywriter in California; and Kara, a dental assistant.

At celebrations when we gather for a family meal, we still sing our traditional blessing to the tune of The Doxology . . . a cappella and in harmony . . . and still hearing Dad's low voice on the "Amen."

> *Be present at our table, Lord*
> *Be here and everywhere adored*
> *These mercies bless and grant that we*
> *May strengthened for Thy service be. AMEN.*

And the legacy goes on. Bompa's great grandchildren are arriving: Liam, Mia, Olive, Silas…

Legacy of Love
From the heart of a grateful grandchild
Words/Music by Sonja Leavitt

Legacy of Love, the thread we pass
Between us; Flesh and Blood

Legacy of Love, the thread we pass
Between us; Life and Love

You tuck me in, kiss my cheek
Sing a song, rock me to sleep

You opened your heart to let me in
My little journey's about to begin

Legacy of Love, the thread we pass
Between us; Flesh and Blood

Legacy of Love, this thread we pass
Between us; Life and Love

You care for me, provide for me
Take pride in me, pray for me

You paved the way, prayed me through
Soon you'll hear me say "I love you"

Days are moving slowly, but life goes so fast
I want every moment spent with you to last

Legacy of Love, the thread we pass
Between us; Flesh and Blood

Legacy of Love, the thread we pass
Between us; Life and Love…

December 29, 2011

It's Daddy's 99th birthday today and I am drawn to take a walk in his honor at Sheldon Marsh, a favorite nature preserve close to our home. I keep my eyes open for geese in the open marsh part of the pathway and then I take the boardwalk that leads to a long stretch of Lake Erie beach. The sun is low in the sky and the clouds full of rosy splendor. I am remembering Dad and thanking God for him and missing him.

The setting sun's gold grows more intense, gilding the trees to my right. Exquisite beauty. I think about the song Sonja wrote in tribute to her Bompa, "The Sun Rises and it Sets." I whisper a prayer: "Lord, may the same Spirit that filled Dad fall on his grandchildren and on his great-grandchildren." As I begin to name them one by one, a gentle rain starts to fall. "Yes, Jesus," I say, "fall like this rain on the generations to follow." Just then, I look up over the lake on my left. And catch my breath. A rainbow is filling the sky above the lake's expanse. God's symbol of promise in response to my prayer is so obvious and so spectacular that it almost strikes me as funny! As many times as I've been to Sheldon Marsh, I have never seen a rainbow in the sky there . . . until today. An exclamation point to end Dad's birthday. I walk to the car in the semi-dark and mist to the overhead sound of . . . honking geese. Of course!

ABOUT THE AUTHOR

Born in Canada and raised in Germany, Donna Gassett came to the United States for her studies at Houghton College (B.A.) and Eastman School of Music (M.A). She traveled extensively in concert ministry with her sisters, Sharon Harder and Darlene Schroeder (Parschauer Sisters) and with her husband, Bill, in Crescendo Ministries.

As singer-songwriter-worship leader, Donna has directed the music at the Chapel in Sandusky, Ohio for the past 15 years.

Donna's spiritual passion permeates the neighborhood Bible study she leads and the women's retreats where she speaks.

Donna and Bill live in Huron, Ohio and have one married musician daughter, Sonja Leavitt. Oh … and a little granddaughter, Olive, one of John Parschauer's great-grandchildren, for whom the story of Bompa was written!

Crescendo Ministries
P.O. Box 494
Huron, OH 44839
E-mail: gassett@bex.net
Telephone: 419-433-8048